SCANNING

THE PROFESSIONAL WAY

SYBIL IHRIG   EMIL IHRIG

Osborne McGraw-Hill

Berkeley   New York   St. Louis   San Francisco
Auckland   Bogotá   Hamburg   London   Madrid
Mexico City   Milan   Montreal   New Delhi   Panama City
Paris   São Paulo   Singapore   Sydney
Tokyo   Toronto

Osborne **McGraw-Hill**
2600 Tenth Street
Berkeley, California 94710
U.S.A.

For information on translations or book distributors outside the U.S.A., or to arrange bulk purchase discounts for sales promotions, premiums, or fundraisers, please contact Osborne **McGraw-Hill** at the above address.

Scanning the Professional Way

67890 DOC 998

ISBN 0-07-882145-2

Publisher:	Lawrence Levitsky
Acquisitions Editor:	Scott Rogers
Project Editor:	Emily Rader
Copy Editor:	Ann Kameoka
Proofreader:	Linda Medoff
Illustrator:	John Wincek
Series Design:	Emil Ihrig, VersaTech Associates
Page Composition:	Sybil Ihrig, VersaTech Associates

About the Authors...

Sybil and Emil Ihrig of VersaTech Associates are prepress and production experts. They are authors of books on several subjects, including CorelDRAW!, QuarkXpress, and PhotoStyler. The Ihrigs currently design and produce books for major publishers throughout the United States. They can be reached on America Online (sybilihrig), on CompuServe (72730,1153), and on the Internet (sybilihrig@aol.com.).

Dedication:

For Herb, Lillian, Alma, Emil Sr., Amy, and Kyle—with love

Contents

iv   Contents

Setting Up a Professional Scanning System   43

Color Fundamentals for Scanning   55

Evaluating Source Images   77

Resolution and Sizing   89

Hands-On Scanning   111

File Formats and Compression   131

Foreword

Those of us who have come from a printing industry background generally maintain a jaded eye toward those who have entered the prepress/printing industry through the "back door" of desktop publishing. The in-the-trenches professionals have an absolute disdain for those who dare to write about the subject.

After all, they got into it the *easy* way. They didn't have to spend years in apprenticeship programs, learning the trade from seasoned master craftsmen. Why, they probably weren't even *born* by the time I was doing day-and-night battle with litho cameras, stripping tables, contact frames, printing presses, and impossible deadlines. They haven't earned the right to speak in behalf of the trade.

They weren't *there* . . . For the most part, they don't have a clue about the in-depth issues of "real litho!" Hrumph! (silent gesture of chest-thumping)

You see, most of us have invested many difficult years in thankless pursuit of excellence. "Good enough is never good enough!" We are all driven, dedicated but rarely recognized . . . unless we fail. The perfect halftone or color separation is surely *the very next one*. This kind of *soul investment* is just about the only thing we hang our pride on. We are *craftsmen*.

Once in a great while we happen upon some individuals who kick the arrogance and hard-earned pride right out from under us— people who may not have come up through the ranks, as we have, but who nevertheless have the same sensitivity and concern about doing printing right!

People like these are hard for us to deal with! However, I've found two that I can deal with. Sybil and Emil Ihrig have taken me off guard. Their candid, in-depth investigation entitled *Scanning the Professional Way* is a serious treatise on how desktop scanners can be used for professional printing results. Although my particular passion is for printing, the Ihrigs also handle production scanning for other applications with aplomb.

I was afforded the privilege of reviewing this book as a technical editor. I have *learned* a lot!

One of the things I was particularly impressed with was the authors' "integrity of intent." What I mean is that, throughout the months that I worked on this project, their attitude remained completely open to the relatively minor corrections that I had to offer. Their research is thorough, their premises are sound, and this work, without a doubt, is the finest I have seen on the subject.

Scanning the Professional Way is a practical guide to digitizing images for the highest-quality results. Don't be deceived by the compactness of this volume; it manages to cover the entire gamut of technical, commercial, and aesthetic concerns related to scanning and does so with great thoroughness and many real-world tips. All of the following issues receive their just dues in this book:

- Matching your input requirements to your output goals
- The technological factors that determine scanning quality
- Types of input devices—drum scanners, film/transparency scanners, flatbed scanners, digital cameras, and Photo CD systems—as well as the characteristics and advantages of each
- Setting up a scanning system that will tackle your typical projects efficiently and avoid bottlenecks
- Color theory and color management as they relate to scanning
- Evaluating source images before scanning to eliminate the "garbage-in, garbage-out" syndrome
- Mastering resolution and sizing so as to maintain image quality from input to final output
- Step-by-step scanning procedures for every kind of original
- File format dos and don'ts

I recommend this book highly to all who desire to produce professional-grade results from desktop scanners, Photo CD, and digital cameras. If I were beginning in (or advancing through) the printing industry, I could ask for no better guide than this. This work *must* be on the shelf of every serious desktop publisher, graphic designer, advertising or marketing communications professional, service bureau or color prepress house employee, print communications professional, and anyone involved with electronic images.

I highly commend this work.

Herb Paynter, President
ImageXpress, Inc.
Atlanta, Georgia
July 1995

Acknowledgments

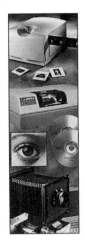

Creating a genuinely useful handbook on digitizing images the professional way demands the support of many individuals and corporations. As compact as the finished product may look, it required what at times seemed like a cast of thousands to produce. We owe thanks to many, many helpers for the information and technical assistance they provided.

First and foremost, we are deeply indebted to publisher Larry Levitsky for his support of our series concept, his openness to many of our design ideas, and his sense of fair play.

Scott Rogers, our editor, is to be commended for his continuing encouragement and for his diplomacy in helping to negotiate many of the issues involved in scheduling and production.

We also want to thank several other Osborne/McGraw-Hill staff with whom we worked closely throughout this project: Daniela Dell'Orco, arguably the most organized and level-headed Editorial Assistant on the planet; Polly Fusco, for her zest and follow-through in building marketing alliances; Patty Mon, for her well-timed publicity efforts; Deborah Wilson, for her able assistance with production issues; and Emily Rader and Ann Kameoka for efficiently coordinating the copy edit.

Herb Paynter of ImageXpress is the most thorough technical editor we've ever had and a highly entertaining one, too ("Just a spoonful of sugar . . ."). Thanks, Herb, for taking time out from your alligator-flogging schedule to canoe your way through the intricacies of our manuscript.

Several scanner manufacturers provided loans of equipment, without which we would have been unable to reproduce many of the images featured in this book. Thanks go to Agfa Division of Bayer for the use of their Vision 35, to Microtek Lab for the ScanMaker III, to Polaroid Corporation for the excellent SprintScan35, to Ron Gustavson at Screen USA for providing drum scans from the DT-1045AI, and to UMAX for the user-friendly PowerLook. We are especially grateful to Polaroid for pulling a rabbit (scanner) out of the hat at the 11th hour. Thanks, Isidro!

Many corporations kindly provided software, product photos, and/or technical information. We would like to express our appreciation to Adobe Systems, Agfa Division of Bayer, DayStar Digital, Dicomed, DPA Software, Eastman Kodak, Electronics for Imaging, the Graphic Arts Technical Foundation, Howtek, Inc., ImageXpress, ImSpace Systems, Light Source Computer Images Inc., Linotype-Hell, Microtek Lab,

Monaco Systems, Nikon Electronic Imaging, Optronics, Pinnacle Micro, Pixelcraft, Polaroid Corporation, R.R. Donnelley & Sons' Prelim department, Radius, Scitex, Screen USA, Second Glance Software, SyQuest Technologies, and UMAX.

There surely are many others to whom we should express our appreciation and whom we've inadvertently omitted due to the chaos of last-minute production—our apologies!

Please accept our thanks for your contributions and our best wishes for the continuing success of *your* enterprises.

We encourage anyone with comments, questions, or suggestions about this book to contact us via electronic mail

Sybil and Emil Ihrig
sybilihrig@aol.com
72730,1153 (CompuServe)

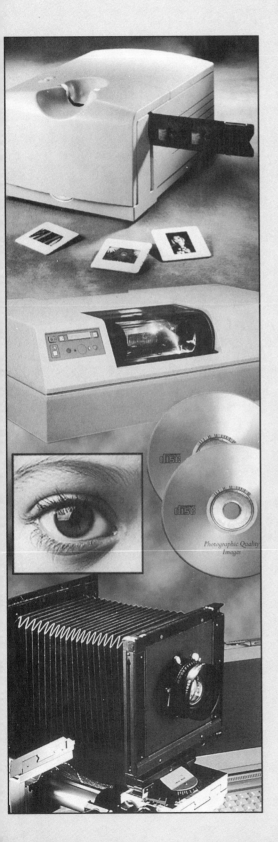

The Ins and Outs of Scanning

When I was about ten years old, a playmate handed me a wooden boomerang. I had heard wild stories about the dangers of this fabled weapon, but, being an adventurous kid, I wanted to find out for myself whether the second-hand tales were true. Effortlessly I flung the boomerang high into the air and so far away that it passed out of visual range. Cool! This was fun! I turned back to my playmate to resume our game. The next thing I knew, I was lying flat on my back on the wet grass with a bloody slash in my forehead, looking confusedly up into the sky and wondering what had hit me.

Novice, intermediate, and (sometimes) even professional-level users of digital scanning devices often suffer a similar plight. Scanners are powerful tools for reproducing real-world images in digital form, and their plug-and-play technologies make the process of capturing visual data seem deceptively simple. Place the artwork face down (if you're using a flatbed scanner), lower the lid, click the Scan button in the plug-in's interface, and go for a cup of coffee. Throw the resulting images into a page layout file, and let's see what comes out.

So far, so good. But when the catalog comes back from the printer with grainy, pixelized product shots and muddy colors, or when the uncompressed legal documents and technical drawings archived with OCR software are too embarrassingly low-resolution to read, it's tempting to feel that the art of scanning is a hit-or-miss affair.

The good news is that there *are* strategies you can follow to ensure high quality for scanned images, whatever your final product. This compact book is full of such strategies. Whether you're scanning images yourself, supervising other employees entrusted with the task, or using the services of an outside vendor, consider this book as a practical roadmap full of clear, detailed signposts that will lead you unerringly to your scanning goals. Some of these signposts include

- Criteria for obtaining quality scans (Chapter 2)
- Types of scanning devices and their characteristics (Chapter 3)
- Building a system that meets your typical scanning needs (Chapter 4)
- Color reproduction and color management basics as they apply to scanning (Chapter 5)
- Evaluating the characteristics of your source images (Chapter 6)
- Determining the right size and resolution (Chapter 7)
- Enhancing images on the fly as you scan (Chapter 8)
- Choosing the right file format in which to save an image (Chapter 9)

The illustrations in the color gallery pages show targeted examples of scanning principles at work. The back of the book contains a handy listing of vendors whose hardware and software products can assist you in achieving quality scanning.

Getting the Terms Straight

When two people set about to communicate with one another, it helps if they are speaking the same language. The field of desktop scanning, like other computer industries, is still so young that many terms get bandied about all too loosely and are used to mean more than one thing. Right up front, let's disperse the fog surrounding the basic terms having to do with the process of scanning and what's being scanned.

Scanning and Image Acquisition

When we use the term *scanning* in these pages, what we really mean is *image acquisition*. Also called *digital input* or *digitization*, image acquisition refers to the process of capturing visual information in a digital form that computers can use. The familiar flatbed, sheet-fed, slide, and drum scanners are not the only devices capable of digitizing images; digital cameras, video capture boards, and Photo CD processing systems can do the job, too. Although we'll be concentrating throughout this book on working with bona fide scanners, we'll also provide tips and tricks for acquiring and using digital photos, video stills, and Photo CD images.

Digital Images, Raster Images

In the computer world, there are basically two types of images: *raster images* and *vector images*. Raster images are produced by paint programs, image editing software, scanners, Photo CD workstations, video capture boards, and digital cameras. They consist of grids of color, grayscale, or black-and-white *pixels* or picture elements. The color characteristics of raster images make them susceptible to humongous file sizes and sensitive to sizing (see the "Pixels, Dots, or Samples?" section in Chapter 2).

Vector images, on the other hand, are made up of mathematical shapes—lines, ellipses, rectangles, curves, and more complex paths—encoded as mathematical formulas. Their streamlined structure keeps file sizes manageable and makes them easy to resize without loss of quality. Computer-based drawing, CAD, 3-D, and tracing programs generate vector images. Figure 1–1 illustrates the major differences between raster and vector images.

Computer graphics and design aficionados tend to use the word *image* to refer to just about everything that's visual—from program interfaces on screen, to digital photos, to artwork created in drawing packages. For purposes of this book, however, the term *digital images* refers only to raster images, which are what scanners and digital cameras produce.

What Comes In Must Go Out

Just as the saying "what goes up must come down" succinctly describes the law of gravity, so "what goes in must come out" sums up an intractable rule of digital image scanning. Yes, this is a book about input, but you also need to have a clear idea of your output goals if you want to be assured of high-quality output results.

In order to make intelligent choices about the hardware, software, and skills needed for your scanning jobs, you have to know as much as possible about the characteristics of both the *source image*—the original to be digitized—and the *output medium* in which your final product will take shape. The source image is generally at hand and easy to examine (see Chapter 6 for guidelines on evaluating source images). However, the scanner operator is often someone other than the person or persons responsible for producing the final product and is therefore less familiar with specialized output requirements.

Common output media for digitized images include print, video, multimedia, and business communications such as fax, e-mail, OCR, and document archival. Each output medium requires its own set of scanning skills.

Figure 1–1   © Emil Ihrig

Raster images (above) consist of grids of individual pixels, while vector images (below) are composed of paths.

Scanning Skills for Print Output

Print output encompasses a broad array of printing devices—black-and-white laser printers, color printers and copiers, imagesetters, as well as web and sheet-fed printing presses. It also includes an even broader range of document types, from in-house newsletters to forms, advertising collateral, magazines, books, posters, and high-end art reproductions. The output requirements for digital images depend heavily on both the document type and printing device.

When you digitize images destined for print output, you need to pay special attention to the following factors:

- Sizing of both the original and the final printed image
- Scanning resolution (or Photo CD resolution when applicable)
- Output resolution, based either on the printer resolution or on the relationship between image resolution and halftone screen frequency
- Range and printability of grayscale or color tones in the scanned image, based on characteristics of the paper and inks to be used
- File format in which to save the digitized image
- Matching scanning device characteristics to the desired level of print quality

Chapters 3, 5, 7, 8, and 9 discuss these considerations in greater detail.

Scanning Skills for Video Output

The fixed color range and screen resolution of video and television differ from those of computer monitors. Resolution and color range standards also differ from one nation to another. In the United States, Canada, Mexico, and Japan, the *NTSC* (National Television Standards Committee) defines these standards; in Europe, an organization called *PAL* sets the specifications. When digitizing an image that will be output to video or television, it's important to

- Know the resolution of your chosen video standard and base the scanning resolution on it
- Know what video editing software will be used to process the images, and its capabilities
- Scan or digitize in 24-bit RGB color
- Save the image in a file format that video, or your particular video editing software, can use

Adjusting the color range of an image to fit video standards is usually a *post-processing* task—one that's best handled in a video editing software package after the image has been digitized.

Scanning Skills for Multimedia Output

The multimedia category includes computer-based corporate presentations, as well as interactive games, animations, educational or training applications, and other software published on disk or CD-ROM. The ultimate multimedia output device is the computer screen, which has a fixed resolution and color set determined by the type of application. Most commercially published games and interactive software use a 256-color palette and a 640 × 480-pixel resolution; corporate presentations can use a larger number of colors and a higher screen resolution if the computer system that is projecting the presentation supports them.

When digitizing images destined for multimedia, be familiar with

- The color palette of either (a) the equipment that will be projecting the presentation or (b) the standard for the interactive software application
- The screen resolution that will be the standard for the presentation or interactive application, stated in horizontal and vertical pixel dimensions

- Any file format requirements dictated by the platform(s) on which the computer-based media will be viewed, or by presentation software or authorware software requirements

Having this information assists you in determining the scanning resolution, scanning color mode, and file format for saving the image (see Chapters 5, 7, and 9). If you disregard these factors, you may waste valuable storage space on unnecessarily large file sizes or need to jettison excess color information at a later time.

Scanning Skills for Business Communications

Beyond graphic arts, video, multimedia, and computer-based presentations, there's a need to digitize information for day-to-day business communications. While the paperless office is not yet a reality, scanning is already an essential element in the creation of the *less*-paper office. Business communications scanning applications include

- *OCR (optical character recognition)* a technology that permits intelligent recognition of text in scanned documents for translating hard-copy documents into text files that can be word processed, then saved, edited, or integrated into another document
- Archiving blueprints, technical drawings, and other vital legal or business documents for long-term storage or for corporate distribution on CD-ROM
- Providing digital news or marketing information that can be faxed, electronically mailed, or distributed on the Internet to staff members, vendors, and customers

The technologies of scanning, fax, electronic mail, and OCR are rapidly converging to such an extent that you can now store and reuse digitally almost any information taken from almost any source. Products that integrate scanning, image editing, OCR, online forms processing, electronic filing, fax, and e-mail functions are heralds of this trend.

Business communications scanning requires many of the same skills as scanning for print publishing and computer-based presentations, except that most of it takes place in black and white or grayscale. Chapters 3, 4, 6, 7, 8, and 9 provide information useful to anyone involved in down-to-earth business scanning.

Scanning Skills for Multipurposed Information

Increasingly, images originally scanned for one type of output eventually need to be reused for one or more additional media. For example, a color photo illustration commissioned for a full-page magazine advertisement may later need to be reincarnated as an opening shot on a corporate video, a background in a computer-based presentation, or a black-and-white logo on a fax cover sheet. This recycling of digital information has been dubbed *multipurposing* by information society pundits.

> **❝***Increasingly, images originally scanned for one type of output eventually need to be reused for one or more additional media.***❞**

If you even remotely suspect that the information you're digitizing might have to be multipurposed at a later date, take these steps to save yourself work and ensure high-quality final output to *every* medium:

1. Scan the original using the "max condition" settings—the scanning mode that reproduces at least 16 million colors in

RGB and the scanning resolution that yields enough information for a large printed image (see Chapters 5 and 7). That way, you won't be caught shy of color or file size should the need for a printed image manifest itself.

2. Avoid enhancing or correcting the color in the image during scanning. An image that has been previously corrected for print reproduction may not have the right color or tonal balance for multimedia or video output.

3. Save this version of the uncorrected image in a TIFF or EPS file format suitable for print publishing, or in the editing software's native file format, which saves images in an economical size (refer to Chapter 9). These formats also contain enough information for later translation to other file formats or other output media.

4. Save another version of the image. Enhance this version for the job at hand and archive the original to serve as a basis for later jobs.

The Right Tools for the Job

So, you know which types of output media you must scan for and which skills must be at your command. Now comes the expensive part: acquiring the computer system, digitizing equipment, and software to carry out your chosen tasks. Following are some suggestions for selecting the optimum hardware and software components based on your scanning requirements. See Chapters 3 and 4 for a more detailed overview of your hardware and software choices.

Hardware

When we discuss hardware in relation to scanning, we're talking about both the scanning equipment itself and the host computer to which the scanning equipment is attached. To avoid frustration and keep the workflow going smoothly, match both components to your output goals.

Scanning Systems for Print Publishing

Print publishing *can* place the heaviest demands on scanning system requirements, but it doesn't have to. Two factors determine the amount of hardware investment you must make: (a) the typical dimensions of printed artwork and (b) whether your projects normally use color or grayscale images. If your projects require mostly black-and-white or duotone images printed at small sizes in newsletters, books, brochures, and the like, you can be well served by a low-end flatbed scanner, a 17-inch monitor, and a moderately fast computer system that includes 8 to 16MB of RAM and a medium-capacity hard drive. A CD-ROM drive for use with Photo CDs is also advisable, and you can take advantage of low-end, low-cost digital cameras such as the Apple QuickTake. On the other hand, projects that feature full-color images at relatively large sizes—particularly for higher-end publications such as glossy magazines, art books, and annual reports—demand 20-inch or larger color monitors, fast computer systems, lots of RAM, large hard drives, CD-ROM drives, and removable storage systems. Scanning options include higher-end flatbed scanners, higher-end digital cameras, in-house drum scanners, or outside vendors that have Pro Photo CD processing systems or drum scanners at their disposal.

Video-Oriented Scanning Systems

Scanning systems that are dedicated to full-motion video production as well as video image capture for video should include a very fast computer, lots of RAM, a 15- or 17-inch color monitor, and removable storage systems. Color flatbed scanners, video capture boards, or still video or low-resolution digital cameras are appropriate digitizing devices. Memory and storage requirements for systems that only capture images and don't need to run authorware are less exacting, since the limited pixel dimensions and small file sizes of single-frame video images don't place heavy demands on the host computer.

Multimedia-Oriented Scanning Systems

This category offers the greatest flexibility in terms of image capture devices, since raw material for computer-based presentations and interactive media can originate from many different sources—screen capture, digital cameras, video capture, Photo CD, and flatbed-scanned artwork. Multimedia design typically specifies 256-color output at a 640 × 480-pixel resolution, which reduces the demands on the display capabilities of the capture system. System speed and RAM must be ample when the system that digitizes source images also runs the authorware to create the final multimedia product.

When the host system is used primarily for presentations, display requirements can be higher and RAM requirements lower than for systems designed to generate interactive software.

Business Communications Scanning Systems

When scanning is geared toward everyday business communications (especially fax, e-mail, and OCR), the CPU speed, RAM, and display requirements of the host computer are not critical. A low-resolution digital camera, a grayscale or low-resolution color flatbed scanner (higher-resolution scanners for long-term document archival), or one of the newer-model multipurpose office communications machines suffices as the capture device. Removable storage media, perhaps on a network server, should be available for OCR and archiving applications.

" Always allow your output needs to guide every phase of your scanning work. "

Scanning Software

Your output goals also help determine the best software for digitizing images. Basically, scanning software falls into three categories: device-specific software, which can include plug-ins compatible with Photoshop and other major image editing packages; OCR packages; and all-in-one, stand-alone scanning utilities.

Plug-ins, once limited in their capabilities, now routinely include functions that allow you to enhance images during scanning and thus minimize data loss (see Chapter 8). They offer the further advantage of allowing users to capture images directly into full-featured image editing packages such as Adobe Photoshop, Micrografx Picture Publisher, Fractal Design Painter, Corel PhotoPaint!, and HSC Live Picture. OCR packages work with many different types of digitizing devices. Stand-alone scanning utilities such as Light Source's Ofoto are good alternatives for those whose supplied plug-ins lack functionality or who want a turnkey scanning and image editing application geared toward very specific output functions. Many higher-end drum scanners offer stand-alone scanning and editing applications which, while device specific, are even more full featured than the major image editing packages.

If you retain only one gem of wisdom from this book, let it be this: Always allow your output needs to guide every phase of your scanning work, from system setup to software selection to image editing functions. That said, let's move ahead to Chapter 2, where we discuss the technological factors that determine quality in image capture.

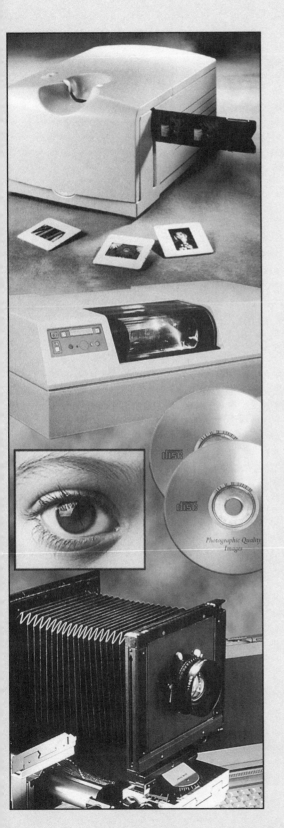

2

Defining Quality in Scanning

In the digital imaging business, it's all too easy to fall prey to techno envy. Advertisements for and reviews of some high-end scanning devices would have you believe that unless you can get your hands on a top-of-the-line drum scanner or digital camera costing hundreds of thousands of dollars, you're a lost soul and your images are not worth the paper (or videotape, or screen) they're output on. Any lesser technology, they claim, produces images that may be "good enough . . . but no cigar."

Don't you believe it.

What defines quality in scanning and image digitization? The technological capabilities of the scanning device as described in this chapter are only one contributing factor. The condition of the source image, the skill of the device operator, and—last but not least—the use to which the final image will be put, all interact with the scanning device technology to determine whether image quality is satisfactory. Not every type of output demands the highest, most expensive level of technology to do the job well. This chapter examines "quality" from the standpoint of the technical capabilities of digitizing devices, always with a view to final output goals. For more information on how source image characteristics and scanning skills help determine image quality, see Chapters 6 and 8, respectively.

Multiple Standards for Quality

For the purposes of this book, a quality scan is one that's good enough to meet all the output requirements of a particular project. An art director for a megabucks magazine advertising campaign has one standard of quality; the publisher of a newsprint-based neighborhood merchant catalog has another; and the producer of an interactive software training package has yet another. All three can obtain "quality" scans using technologies that differ greatly from one another in terms of pricing and capabilities.

Satisfactory image captures result from a successful match between the capabilities of the digitzing device and the output requirements of the end user. From the standpoint of equipment, criteria affecting input quality include sensing technology, input and optical resolution, enlargement factor, imaging area, bit depth, and dynamic and density ranges, all of which we'll define and explore in this chapter.

Note: *In digital cameras, the quality of the optical system is an additional factor determining the quality of image capture.*

Sensing Technology

All digitizing equipment commercially available today uses one of two types of light-sensing devices: *charge-coupled devices* (*CCDs*) or *photomultiplier tubes* (*PMTs*). In addition, all scanning devices use *analog-to-digital converters* (*A/D converters*) to translate the sensed information into digital data.

Charge-Coupled Devices (CCDs)

Flatbed, sheet-fed, and hand-held scanners, dedicated film and slide scanners, and still video and digital cameras use CCDs to sense light levels. A CCD is a solid-state electronic element composed of multiple tiny sensors, which can register an analog electrical charge proportional to the intensity of light falling on it. CCDs have various configurations depending on the type of scanner. In flatbed scanners, CCD component sensors are arranged in one row (for three-pass scanning) or three rows on a chip (for single-pass scanning), as shown in Figure 2–1. This arrangement allows the device to sample the entire width of an analog original image and record it as a complete line. Each time the CCD samples a line of the original image, it sends the charges (representing analog light levels) to the A/D converters to be translated into binary data. The CCD is now free to receive electrical charges from the next line. This process takes only a small fraction of a second in newer scanners.

Note: *In slide scanners, digital and video cameras, CCD sensors are typically arranged in a rectangular array so that information can be captured as a simultaneous block rather than one scan line at a time.*

CCD designs vary in their sensitivity to light levels and to extraneous electrical noise. These factors are discussed more fully in the "Resolution" and "Dynamic Range, Density Range" sections of this chapter. They can affect the resolution of which the scanning device is capable, the range of color and gray tones the scanning device can register, and the accuracy of the color or grayscale information detected. Cheaper scanning devices tend to use lower quality CCDs than their higher-end counterparts. The more expensive CCDs found in professional-quality flatbeds, slide scanners, and higher-end digital cameras yield better quality image input.

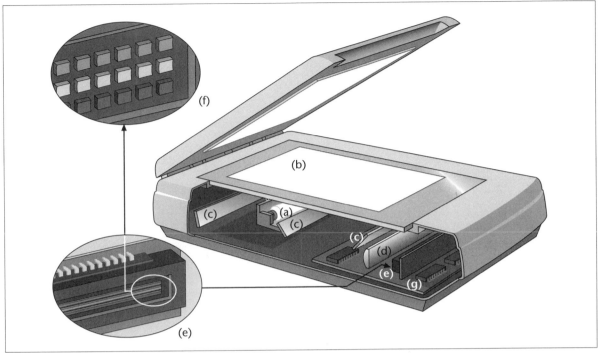

Figure 2–1

*CCDs at work in a typical flatbed scanner. A light source (**a**) reflects light off the original artwork (**b**). Mirrors (**c**) relay the reflected light to the lens (**d**), which focuses the image information onto the CCD chip (**e**, inset **e**) containing either one or three rows of sensors (inset **f**). The CCD registers the light as analog voltage charges, which it then directs to the A/D converters (**g**) for conversion to digital data.*

Photomultiplier Tubes (PMTs)

Drum scanners of all types (see Chapter 3) use photomultiplier tubes (PMTs) instead of CCDs as light-sensing devices. PMTs are based on an older vacuum-tube technology which, while more expensive to maintain than the newer CCD technology, has proven its quality and reliability.

In typical drum scanners that have three PMTs (one each for red, green, and blue), a xenon or tungsten-halogen light source focuses on an extremely small area of the original using fiber optics and condenser lenses. (Figure 2–2 shows a transparency lit from the inside of the drum; reflective materials are lit from the outside.) Light transmitted or reflected from the image is then projected onto angled, partially transparent mirrors as shown in Figure 2–2. Each mirror reflects some of the light and transmits some to the next mirror. The reflected portion of the mirrored light passes through the appropriate color filter and thence into the corresponding PMT, where a process known as *optical amplification* takes place. Electrons emitted when light strikes the cathode of the PMT travel through layers of dynodes, which emit additional electrons, thus amplifying them to the point at which the light can be converted into electrical signals. The anode of the PMT measures analog variations in these signals, which then travel to the A/D converters to be registered as digital data.

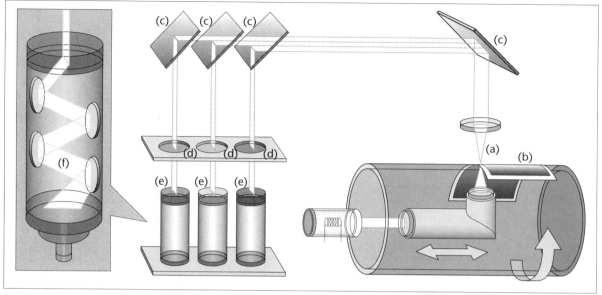

Figure 2–2

*PMT technology at work. Light (**a**) projected onto an original (**b**) is reflected and transmitted from semi-transparent mirrors (**c**), travels to the red, green, or blue filter (**d**), and passes into the corresponding PMT (**e**). Inside the PMT (**inset**), light (**f**) is amplified through secondary emission until it is converted into electrical signals, which the A/D converters then translate into digital signals. Many drum scanners include a fourth PMT to capture sharpening information.*

PMT technology permits capture of the broadest possible range of tones with high fidelity. Until very recently, in fact, all CCD-based devices were considered inherently inferior to PMT-based drum scanners in terms of the image quality that could be achieved. Continuing improvements in CCD and A/D converter technology have eliminated many perceived CCD shortcomings, and some experts maintain that higher-end CCD-based scanners can now reproduce images with fidelity similar to that of drum scanners. Chapter 3 addresses that ongoing debate in more detail.

A/D Converters and Processors

Analog-to-digital converters play a major role in the quality of the digital signals that become the image on your monitor. Their task is to process the continuously variable analog voltage read-

ings sensed by the CCDs or PMTs into numbers that represent color or grayscale values. Both the number of colors and the level of detail that a scanner can capture are linked to the sensitivity of its A/D converters. As you might expect, the lower the cost of the scanner, the less sensitive its A/D converters are likely to be.

Desktop drum scanners and many midrange and higher-end flatbed scanners use additional processors, such as *digital signal processors* (*DSPs*) to increase scanning speed and perform other image processing tasks on the fly.

Resolution

If commonly used words in the electronic publishing field were actors, the term "resolution" would be awarded an Oscar for versatility. Input resolution, scanning resolution, optical resolution, interpolated resolution, screen (monitor) resolution, image resolution, output resolution—these are just some of the many masks this character wears. In fact, resolution has such a starring role in digital scanning and output that we devote all of Chapter 7 to it.

Here, our main concern is with two types of resolution that affect scanning quality: *input resolution* (also known as *scanning resolution*) and *optical resolution*. We'll briefly review some other meanings of the term "resolution" just to help you keep on the straight and narrow path of scanning.

Input Resolution

All digitizing devices—scanners, digital and video cameras, and Photo CD workstations—have several functions in common:

- They translate *analog* (real-world) information into digital data that a computer can use.
- They generate raster images, which are composed of grids of black-and-white, grayscale, or colored *pixels* (picture elements).

Note: *Raster images are often called bitmapped images, but there's an important difference between the two. The term* raster images *encompasses all pixel-based images, regardless of their color characteristics.* Bitmapped images *contain black-and-white pixels only.*

- They sense or *sample* the original image at frequent intervals, checking the grayscale or color value at each *sample point*.

A scanner's *input resolution* simply measures the density at which a scanning device samples information within a given amount of space (usually per inch or per centimeter) during the digitization process. Although input resolution is one determinant of scanning quality, the popular wisdom that says that higher input resolution

automatically leads to higher-quality images doesn't necessarily hold true. As you'll see in Chapter 7, what's essential is having exactly the right amount of digital *information* in an image. And in order to determine how much information is just right, you need to coordinate input resolution with both the size of the original image and the desired output size. (For print output, you also need to know the halftone screen frequency, measured in lines per inch or *lpi*.)

Pixels, Dots, or Samples?

There's considerable confusion over the correct term to use when measuring input resolution for scanning devices. This confusion has arisen largely because a single term often describes more than one thing in the desktop publishing and multimedia fields. The most common terms you're likely to encounter are *ppi*, *spi*, and *dpi*.

PPI (pixels per inch)

The word "pixels" can describe several different phenomena: the density of information that a scanning device can capture per inch (*input* or *scanning resolution*), the total amount of information in a raster image (*image resolution*), and the number of discrete horizontal and visual elements that a computer monitor can display at one time (*screen resolution*). It's important to distinguish between these various usages.

The software interfaces for many digitizing devices describe sampling rates in *ppi* or *pixels per inch*. Whereas many digital and still video cameras have a single, fixed input resolution, scanners usually offer a variable range of resolutions from which to choose. But as the sampling rate of a scanning device increases, the size of the pixels it generates decreases (Figure 2–3). You can easily understand why if you imagine trying to pack 50 sardines into a can meant for only 25 standard-sized sardines. The 50 sardines will fit only if they're twice as small as the standard 25.

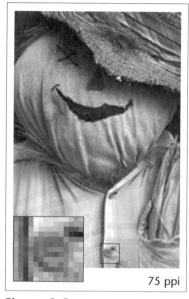

75 ppi   150 ppi   300 ppi

Figure 2–3

© Emil Ihrig

Pixel size decreases as input resolution (scanning resolution) increases.

The term "pixels" also can indicate the total amount of information a digitized image contains in its horizontal and vertical dimensions (800 × 400 pixels, for example). This usage describes *image resolution* rather than input resolution (see Chapter 7). Finally, many people use the term pixels to describe *screen resolution*, the discrete number of horizontal and vertical visual elements that a computer monitor can display—1024 × 768 pixels, for example. The size of pixels on a computer monitor, unlike the size of pixels captured by a scanning device, remains constant. A monitor, therefore, displays all pixels from every image at a single fixed size. This explains why an image scanned at 300 ppi displays at only 72 ppi on a Macintosh monitor and looks much bigger on screen than it would in print.

SPI (samples per inch)

Purists may be correct when they claim that the term "samples," not "pixels," should be used to describe what scanning devices are sensing and reproducing. Still, the ppi nomenclature has so

ingrained itself in the scanning industry that we know better than to think that a few voices crying in the wilderness can turn this historical usage around. Just keep the different meanings of the word "pixels" in mind when scanning.

DPI (dots per inch)

Many journalists and some scanning software interfaces (Figure 2–4) still use the term *dpi* (*dots per inch*) to describe scanning or input resolution. Technically, however, *dots per inch* refers to *output resolution*, the horizontal density of the marks that imagesetters and PostScript laser printers make during the output process. Take care not to confuse the two—think "ppi" whenever you see "dpi" in a scanner interface.

Optical Resolution Versus Interpolated Resolution

One of your top criteria when selecting a scanner or filmless camera should be the maximum input resolution of a particular scanning

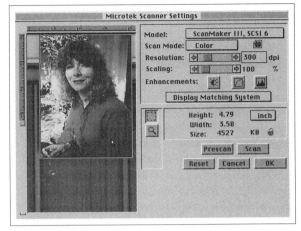

Figure 2–4

Input resolution is often measured in dpi (dots per inch), as in this dialog box for the Microtek ScanMaker III flatbed scanner.

device. Manufacturers define this maximum in two ways: as *optical resolution* or as *interpolated resolution*.

Optical Resolution

Optical resolution describes the amount of actual information a device's optical system can sample. The factors that define optical resolution vary according to the type of digitizing device. In flatbed, sheet-fed, hand-held, and many slide or transparency scanners, maximum optical resolution depends on two factors: the number of individual sensors in the linear CCD(s) arranged within the moving scan head, and the width of the largest original that the scanner can accept. For example, a 5,100-cell CCD array in a scanner that accepts originals up to 8.5 inches wide yields a maximum horizontal optical resolution of 600 ppi. The distance a scan head travels past the original artwork determines the vertical resolution, which can be higher than the horizontal optical resolution. Digital and still video cameras and some transparency scanners typically use a rectangular CCD array (not a moving linear

one) that fixes the total number of pixels they can capture in either dimension. In drum scanners, the speed of rotation, the brightness of the light source, the stepping motor's capabilities, and the size of the lens aperture combine to determine the maximum optical resolution.

Note: *Flatbed scanner manufacturers often advertise a vertical optical resolution that's twice as high as the horizontal resolution, such as 600 × 1200 ppi. The transport mechanism of these scanners takes "half steps," moving forward one-half pixel at a time, with the result that pixels overlap. To derive the final color or gray values, the scanner must perform mathematical averaging. The "true" optical resolution for these scanners is the lower number (600 × 600 ppi, for example), which also delivers the best results in terms of clarity and reduced noise.*

Interpolated Resolution

A device's maximum *interpolated resolution*, on the other hand, represents the *apparent* amount of information that a scanner can capture with the added help of processor- and/or software-based algorithms. Interpolation algorithms don't add new detail; they merely average the color or grayscale data of adjoining pixels, adding a new pixel in between. Interpolated resolution is often two or more times higher than the optical resolution. Figure 2–5 compares the results of scanning at maximum optical resolution with scanning at maximum interpolated resolution.

Beware of marketing hype—where quality is an issue, only optical resolution counts. Interpolation adds "pseudo" information that may be adequate for low-budget publications or comps, but which will never do for larger-format color images where intricate detail and broad tonal range are vital. Interpolation also tends to soften an image and make more sharpening necessary. If you scan frequently for demanding print applications, you're better off

Figure 2–5

© Emil Ihrig

The image on the left was scanned at a flatbed's maximum optical resolution (300 ppi), while the image on the right was scanned at an interpolated resolution of 600 ppi. Both images were then resized to a common output resolution for printing. A comparison of close-ups reveals that scanners' interpolation algorithms add pixels without adding true detail.

spending extra money on a scanner with a higher optical resolution.

Enlargement Factor

Enlargement factor refers to the number of times the original artwork must be magnified during scanning to achieve the desired output size. If you primarily scan small originals (such as slides and transparencies) that you want to print at much larger sizes, you need all the uninterpolated data you can get. This is possible only with very high-resolution devices such as slide scanners

and drum scanners. The software that accompanies most drum scanners automatically calculates the required input resolution, based on the size of the original and your desired enlargement factor. You need to perform this calculation manually for many flatbed and slide scanners.

Imaging Area

The size of the largest original that a device can digitize determines the device's *imaging area*, also called its *effective scanning area*. Hand-held scanners are low-cost in part because their imaging areas are limited. Flatbed scanners typically feature maximum imaging areas ranging from 8.5 × 11 inches to 11 × 17 inches. Slide and transparency scanners have fixed imaging areas based on standard film or transparency sizes, though some models adapt to multiple media sizes. The imaging areas of drum scanners vary from 8×10 inches at the low end to 20×25 inches at the high end. Filmless cameras are essentially scanners for 3-D objects—the terminology of camera optics applies better to them than discussions of imaging area.

Together, imaging area, optical resolution, and source image dimensions limit the maximum number of pixels that a scanning device can sample and the maximum size at which the resulting digital image can be printed (see Chapter 7).

Bit Depth, Color Depth

Bit depth and *color depth* express, in powers of two, the maximum number of color or gray levels a scanning device can sense for each pixel that it samples. A one-bit scanner (or a color or grayscale scanner in black-and-white mode) reproduces all tones in the original image as either black or white ($2^1 = 2$ levels). An 8-bit grayscale scanner can theoretically capture 2^8 or 256 different levels of gray. And a 24-bit color scanner samples eight bits per pixel for *each* of the three RGB color channels, for a total of $256 \times 256 \times 256 = 16,777,216$ (2^{24}) possible color values. Figure C–1 in the color gallery illustrates the relationship between bit depth and the number of possible color or gray levels in a digitized image.

As bit depth increases, so does the amount of detail that a scanning device can capture, at least theoretically. Twenty-four bit RGB "true" color has become a standard for scanning and image editing, in part because the magic number 256 corresponds to the maximum number of light levels per color channel that PostScript—the digital standard for print publishing—can reproduce.

When comparing scanning devices, however, not all bits are equal. In CCD-based devices, the upper two bits of the device's theoretical color depth are generally "garbage" bits that don't yield accurate color information. That is,

the first six bits (64 colors per channel, or 262,144 colors) are reliable, but the last 198 colors per channel are progressively less so. Inherent limitations of some CCD designs are responsible for this shortcoming:

- Less expensive CCDs are sensitive to ambient electrical noise, which can distort an otherwise "pure" color reading. On the other hand, CCDs used in higher-end flatbeds, slide scanners, and digital cameras feature a much higher *signal-to-noise ratio* and thus can transmit purer signals to the A/D converters.

- There's a built-in tradeoff between CCD size and light sensitivity. Think of CCDs as water buckets: the smaller the bucket, the less water it can hold. In order to obtain higher optical resolutions, manufacturers must pack smaller-size CCDs together. The smaller the individual elements, the narrower the range of light levels that each one can distinguish. When the original to be digitized contains a full range of tones from white to black, the CCDs' ability to capture all the detail is compromised. The "Dynamic Range, Density Range" section of this chapter explains the consequences in greater detail.

- CCDs are also subject to a phenomenon called *crosstalk*. To better understand crosstalk, imagine walking from a dark house out into a snowy landscape. The intense brightness hurts your eyes, temporarily blinding you so that you can't easily perceive the subtle transitions between light levels in the landscape. In the same way, crosstalk occurs when light saturates densely packed adjacent CCD elements, distorting the purity of the signals that each individual cell is supposed to "see." Neighboring pixels in the digitized image experience some mutual color corruption as a result.

The most obvious result of the "garbage" bits phenomenon is that images digitized using lower-end CCD-based devices often lack the continuous, smooth transitions between adjacent light levels that their nominal bit depth would lead you to believe they should have. Scanner and filmless camera manufacturers have come up with several workarounds to this problem, such as devices that sense higher bit depths per channel (10, 12, 14, or even 16). The garbage bits can be thrown away, leaving 256 clean(er) tones per color channel in the final digitized image. This brings us to a discussion of dynamic range, a factor that is closely related to bit depth as a yardstick of scanning quality.

Dynamic Range, Density Range

Whereas bit depth determines the total number of raw color or gray levels that a scanning device can detect, *dynamic range* (sometimes called *density range*) determines the smoothness of the *transitions* between adjacent tones in a digitized image. These terms can apply to originals as well as to scanning devices. When applied to originals, density range is measured as a value between 0 and 4 *OD* (*optical density*), which refers to light blocking capability in transparent originals or light absorbing capability in reflective originals. When applied to digitizing devices, dynamic range describes the device's ability to reproduce subtle changes in tone and expresses the difference between the lightest tones (*dmin*) and the darkest tones (*dmax*) that a given device can sense. As the dynamic range or density value of a scanner or an original increases, so does the range of light levels that it can sense, block, or absorb. The broader a device's dynamic range, the more visible detail it can capture. This is especially true of the shadows (the darkest areas), where it's most difficult to sample detail accurately

because of the limited amount of light energy available to reflect or transmit shadow detail.

Figure 2–6 shows how dynamic range affects the content of a digitized image. The top image, scanned from a photographic print using an older model flatbed scanner, shows obvious tonal compression in the shadows and some compression in the highlights. The bottom image, scanned using a newer model flatbed that features a much higher dynamic range, shows more subtle detail in the shadow and highlight areas. Dynamic range can vary, even among scanning devices with the same nominal bit depth, so when purchasing a device, research the issue carefully and obtain sample images for comparison purposes. You should also keep in mind that dynamic range is not the sole determinant of scanning quality; a scanner that uses noisy CCD sensors can still produce "dirty" scans, no matter how high a dynamic range it boasts.

Both scanning devices and the original media they digitize have density characteristics, as shown in Table 2–1. Generally, drum scanners feature higher dynamic ranges and dmax values than most other types of digitizing devices, and *transmissive* media (film, slides, and transparencies) have broader dynamic ranges and higher dmax values than *reflective* media (photographic prints and paper-based images). Another factor that affects dynamic range in scanning is the logarithmic (nonlinear) nature of density. Scanned positives (reflective prints, slides, hand-drawn artwork) tend to show more tonal compression in the shadows, while scanned negatives (negative film and transparencies) show the most compression in the highlight areas. No input device can compensate 100 percent for this tendency, but broad dynamic ranges certainly help minimize such compression.

To obtain the highest quality scan, select an input device for which both dynamic range *and* dmax match or exceed those of the most demanding media you digitize regularly. For example, a midrange flatbed scanner with a dynamic range of 3.0 and a dmax of 3.2 can easily capture all the tones in reflective photographic prints. The same scanner, if equipped with a transparency adapter, can also adequately capture the tonal information in most commercial grade color slides. But to capture all the information in duplicate slides and in the highest grade transparency films used in big-budget advertising, a drum scanner or very high-end flatbed would be required. If you don't need to digitize the high-end media very often, you don't need to spend the extra money on a corresponding high-end device. That also holds true if you usually output to uncoated papers or newsprint, which severely limit the reproducible tonal range.

Tip: *Manufacturers of low-end and midrange input devices usually don't specify dynamic range and dmax values for their equipment. Research this issue when considering the purchase of an input device, and encourage manufacturers to list dmax, dmin, and dynamic range on their specification sheets.*

Improving Dynamic Range

Recent advances in scanner and digital camera design have contributed industry wide to improved dynamic ranges. Some of these advances include the following:

- **Scanners with higher bit depths**—Newer model CCD-based devices can capture 10, 12, or even 16 raw bits per color channel, thanks to improved sensitivities of the CCDs themselves. The A/D converters on these devices have the processing power necessary to throw out the upper garbage bits and sample the raw analog voltages down to 8 good, and relatively clean bits of useful tonal data per color.

- **CCDs with higher signal-to-noise ratios**—The more expensive CCDs used in higher-end flatbeds, slide/transparency scanners, and digital cameras are more resistant to electrical noise sources (overhead lights, ambient radio waves, and so on). This reduces crosstalk and leads to purer analog voltage signals, which in turn are converted to cleaner tonal detail.

- **On-the-fly tonal correction**—Digital signal processing (DSP) chips and adaptive A/D converters on some

Figure 2–6   © Emil Ihrig

*Dynamic range affects the smoothness of transitions and level of detail in a digitized image. **Top:** An image scanned using equipment with a low dynamic range lacks detail at the tonal extremes; shadows are compressed to black. **Bottom:** The same image scanned using equipment with a higher dynamic range shows significantly better detail in both shadows and highlights.*

Device/Media	Typical Dynamic or Density Range
Input Devices	
Hand-held scanners	2.2 or below
Grayscale scanners and multipurpose devices	2.5 or below
Color flatbed scanners, older models and low-end	2.0 to 2.5
Color flatbed scanners, midrange	2.8 to 3.2
Color flatbed scanners, high-end	3.4 to 3.9
Drum scanners, desktop	3.4 to 4.0
Drum scanners, high-end	3.6 to 4.0
Digital cameras	Depends on ISO rating—see Chapter 3
Still video cameras	Depends on ISO rating
Master and Pro Photo CD workstations	2.8
Source Media	
Artwork on newsprint	0.9
Artwork on coated stock	1.5 to 1.9
Photographic prints	2.3
Negative films	2.8
Commercial-grade color slides	2.7 to 3.0
High-grade transparencies, slide films, and dupes	3.0 to 4.0

Table 2–1

Typical Dynamic Ranges of Scanning Devices and Density Ranges of Original Media

scanning devices make it possible to optimize image tones *before* the analog light levels are converted to digital color values. These developments help alleviate the inevitable data loss that occurs when tonal correction takes place *after* scanning.

- **Adjustable exposure controls**—Desktop drum scanners and some digital cameras and slide scanners let you change exposure and aperture settings. If the scanner's bit depth is high enough, a combination of narrower aperture, higher gamma value setting, and longer exposure time permits capture of more detail in those critical shadow tones.

Provided your scanning software supports it, there are also image correction techniques you can use during scanning to improve an image's dynamic range. Chapters 6 and 8 discuss these in more detail.

We all want the best quality possible in our digital images. In this chapter, we've taken a look at the leading technological factors that contribute to input quality—sensing technology, input and optical resolution, enlargement factor, imaging area, bit depth, and dynamic range. In the next chapter, we'll see how these technologies apply to specific types of digitizing devices.

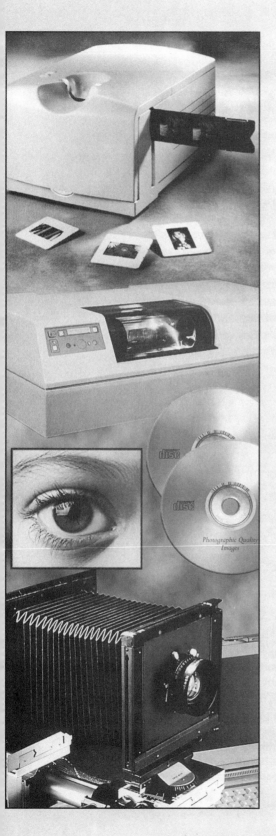

3

Types of Scanning Devices

J ust as there's more than one way to skin a cat, so there's more than one way to get images into a computer. In fact, the number and variety of digitizing options available today seem little short of bewildering. Should you send out for drum scans? Buy your own flatbed scanner? Bring a dedicated film or transparency scanner in-house? Have slides and negatives transferred to Photo CD? Use a digital camera? And, heavens, will your chosen input device produce results that are good enough?

The issues need not be that complex. Choosing an appropriate input source is a matter of matching four factors:

- Characteristics of the source image (see Chapter 6)
- Final output needs
- Technological factors that determine scanning quality (see Chapter 2)
- Capabilities of each type of scanning device

In this chapter, we'll explore the capabilities, uses, and limitations of each type of digitizing device commonly used today. We'll also examine how sensing technology, optical resolution, enlargement capabilities, color depth, dynamic range, and other factors determine the best input and output applications for each device class.

Drum Scanners

Of all the possible applications for scanned images—print, presentations, multimedia, business communications, video—color print publishing is admittedly the most demanding. This is especially true for color prepress houses, big-budget advertising professionals, and publishers of Fortune 500 annual reports, fine art books, and glossy magazines. These professionals place a premium on quick turnaround, high-volume scanning, and critical quality control. For this market, *rotary drum scanners* have always defined the standard of high-end scanning quality. Until very recently, however, the proprietary nature of the technology and the elephantine size of the equipment, combined with the skill levels required for operation and prohibitive cost ($200,000 and upward, not counting maintenance) conspired to make the benefits of rotary drum scanning unavailable to all but the deepest pockets. Other print publishing professionals could obtain expensive scans from these wondrous machines only by sending out to a specialized color separation house.

High-end scanning has been democratized over the past couple of years by the advent of "baby" drums—rotary drum scanners sized down to fit the desktop and connecting to a Macintosh, Windows-based PC, or UNIX workstation. These open-platform devices retain many of the productivity-enhancing features and all of the image reproduction quality of their "big drum" cousins, but at a fraction of the cost. Small service bureaus, corporate marketing, advertising, publishing professionals, and medium-budget magazine publishers now have cause to rejoice at the new accessibility of drum scanning quality—even though not everyone agrees that drum scanners are inherently superior to flatbeds (see "The Drum Versus Flatbed Issue" later in this chapter).

> **"** *High-end scanning has been democratized by the advent of 'baby' drums.* **"**

What's in a Drum?

Desktop drum scanners share with their high-end counterparts a design technology that contributes to high-fidelity color and grayscale image reproduction. The basic principles of drum scanning are straightforward. Artwork is taped, powdered, or oiled down onto the outside of a clear Plexiglas cylinder, the *drum*, which is supported by a heavy base that gives it superb stability. The drum rotates at high speeds (typically 300 to 1,350 rpm) around a scanning sensor unit just a few millimeters away. Within the sensor unit, an extremely bright halogen or xenon fixed light source directs light first to the artwork—sampling the media one pixel at a time through a tiny, cone-like aperture—and then to angled mirrors and RGB filters that split the light into three beams. (The sensor unit lights transmissive originals from the inside of the drum and reflective materials from the outside.) Photomultiplier tubes (PMTs) in the sensor unit receive and amplify the mirrored and filtered light (see Figure 2–2 in Chapter 2). A/D converters then translate these analog signals into digital ones.

Several advantages contribute to the lure of the drum scanner:

- **High color depth and broad dynamic range**—Drum scanners typically sample 10 to 16 bits of color per channel (30- to 48-bit color) and boast dynamic ranges of 3.6 to 4.0 and dmax values of 3.7 to 4.0. These features allow them to capture an extremely broad range of tones, resulting in outstanding detail even in shadow areas. The high rotational speeds of rotary drum mechanisms make it possible to focus an extremely strong light source on the artwork without damaging media. The strength of this light source, combined with variable focusing and the one-pixel-at-a-time sampling methodology, guarantee a high signal-to-noise ratio, which in turn allows the light to sample all the tones in an image accurately without crosstalk from neighboring pixels. Accurate sampling ensures that the analog voltages amplified by the PMTs provide correct data to the A/D converters and processors. Figure C–2 in the color gallery compares the shadow detail of a drum-scanned image with the same image scanned using a good-quality 35mm slide scanner.

- **High resolution and enlargement capabilities**—Pixel-by-pixel sampling means that the optical resolution of drum scanners is limited only by the maximum size of the drum and the minimum size of the aperture. Extremely high optical resolutions (2,500 to 8,000 ppi depending on model) are therefore common. These high resolutions make it feasible to magnify small originals (such as slides and transparencies) many times without loss of quality or detail.

- **Multiple-media flexibility**—Drum scanners can accept slides, transparencies, negative film (in some cases), prints, hand-drawn artwork—in fact, any type of transmissive or reflective medium that is flexible enough to be attached to the drum.

- **Productivity-enhancement features**—Service bureaus, ad agencies, and professionals who have high-volume scanning needs look for features that increase throughput and cost-effectiveness. Depending on the model, drum scanners offer many such productivity-enhancing features. *Batch scanning* allows the operator to scan multiple originals at one time, saving each image into a separate file. *Automatic media sensing* and *motorized refocusing* permit unattended scanning of multiple media of varying densities. Removable drums offered on some models are a time-saver that allows one group of originals to be mounted on a second drum while the first is spinning. Finally, many drum scanners perform *on-the-fly* prepress image enhancement functions such as unsharp masking (using a fourth PMT), color balancing, undercolor removal (UCR), gray component replacement (GCR), and RGB-to-CMYK conversion. On-the-fly processing preserves color integrity, since it is performed on raw analog data *before* the file is sampled down to 24-bit color and saved.

High-end and desktop drum scanners share similar rotary-drum designs, PMT-based image sampling technologies, and broad dynamic ranges. Yet they also differ in other terms besides cost. Let's take a look at the factors that make each type suitable for a particular market segment.

High-End Drum Scanners

The term "high-end" in drum scanning used to be reserved for proprietary turnkey systems from manufacturers like Linotype-Hell, Scitex, Dupont Crosfield, and Dainippon Screen. Although these manufacturers continue to dominate the field, closed-loop systems seem to be gradually heading the way of dinosaurs as desktop-based systems gain the ascendancy. Even at the high end of the market, manufacturers of top-flight scanners are scrambling to integrate the PostScript capability and Macintosh or PC connectivity that desktop-based publishing professionals want. The demands for modularity and upgradability are redefining the high end of drum scanning even at service bureaus and dedicated color prepress houses.

High-end drum scanners such as those pictured in Figures 3–1 and 3–2 offer several features that distin-guish them from their desktop-based relatives and make them suitable for the truly high-volume color scanning work environment:

- **Onboard computer**—High-end drums can achieve excellent hourly throughput because the processing takes place in the scanner's onboard computer, rather than relying on the resources of the host computer as with desktop models.

- **Proprietary software**—Stand-alone software packages provided with high-end drum scanners offer many automated enhancement functions and *presets*—sets of image processing operations that can be applied auto-matically to scans of a similar type. They also have their own learning curves.

- **Resolution, drum size, rotational speed**—High-end scanners offer input resolutions of 8,000 ppi or higher, drum sizes that accept original media in the 20 × 25-inch range, and top rotational speeds of 1,200 rpm or higher.

- **Training, maintenance, cost**—The high-end drums carry price tags in the $60,000 to $200,000 range. Ongoing maintenance tends to be costly, and manufacturer-sponsored training is also important to assist operators in acquiring and maintaining the skills needed to milk the most from the feature set. Top-end scanners aren't as intimidating as they used to be in the days of proprietary systems, but there's more to the process than setting up a toaster.

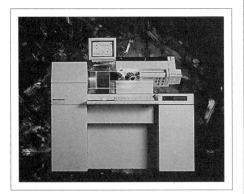

Figure 3–1   *courtesy Linotype-Hell*

The Linotype-Hell ChromaGraph 3900 offers productivity enhancements such as a high-speed mode, a 3,000 percent enlargement factor, a maximum scan area of 20 x 25.6 inches, and automatic recognition of multiple drums.

Figure 3–2   *courtesy Screen USA*

Dainippon Screen's DT-S1045AI includes an on-board 24-channel color computer and an automated setup assistance program that uses artificial intelligence to analyze images and select the proper settings for optimum reproduction.

Desktop "Baby" Drums

Costing between $13,000 to $60,000, the new breed of "baby" drum scanners is particularly attractive to ad agencies, marketing communications departments, ser-vice bureaus and full-service print houses, and other print publishing environments where near-instant turnaround is as important an issue as quality. When rush jobs and last-minute changes are the norm, having a drum scan-ner in-house can be a real cost saver. Birmy Graphics Corporation, DuPont Crosfield, Howtek, Itek, Optronics, ScanView, and Dainippon Screen now have small foot-print drum scanners available, and the list of manufacturers is growing.

The feature sets of "baby" drums vary to target the needs of specific market segments (see Figures 3–3 and 3–4). At the low end, you'll find optical resolutions of 2,500 ppi, dynamic ranges of 3.6 (still superior to that of most flatbed scanners), and few automated features. At the high end, optical resolutions of 8,000 ppi, density ranges at or near 4.0, and fully automated batch scanning and image processing rival the capabilities of stand-alone drum scanners. Desktop models do offer smaller drum sizes than their high-end cousins, but studies show that most original artwork fits within the 11 × 15-inch imaging area that more expensive "baby" drums can accommodate. For the occasional oversized original that won't fit on the in-house desktop drum, you can always send out to the "big" drum at a color prepress house.

The gap in feature sets between small-footprint and high-end drum scanners is rapidly narrowing. Here's an overview of especially noteworthy desktop drum capabilities:

- **Batch scanning**—All desktop models can accommodate both reflective and transmissive artwork of varying densities on the same drum, and several models can automatically adjust aperture and illumination to match the density of each original. For many models, optional software is available that permits input of separate setup parameters for each original on the drum. These features make unattended scanning of multiple originals possible and greatly enhance throughput.

- **Removable drums**—Another productivity-enhancing feature is the use of removable drums for all but the lowest-end desktop models. To save time, you can mount a second set of originals on a spare drum while the first one is scanning. If your model includes automated job control software, you can even interrupt a job, remove the drum to insert a rush project, and automatically resume the original scanning job once the emergency is over.

- **Optional software**—Whereas high-end drum scanners come equipped with stand-alone software, most desktop models include only a Macintosh or Windows Photoshop-compatible plug-in as standard. To get the most from productivity-enhancement features such as automated on-the-fly sharpening, RGB-to-CMYK conversion, color enhancement, and descreening, you often need to purchase expensive optional software.

Figure 3–3   *courtesy Screen USA*

Screen USA's DT-S1015, aimed at lower-volume drum scanning users, omits the removable drum but features 2,500-ppi resolution, 30-bit color sensing, a 5.8 x 5.9-inch imaging area, and optional intelligent scanning setup software.

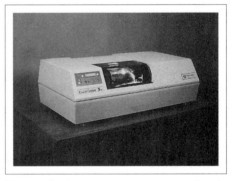

Figure 3–4   *courtesy Optronics*

The Optronics ColorGetter III Pro rivals high-end drum scanner capabilities, offering 8,000 ppi resolution, a 4.0 dynamic range, and automated media sensing. It accepts media up to 11 x 15 inches in size.

Flatbed Scanners

Flatbed scanners are the workhorses of the industry and the most popular type of input device. And with good reason: they're affordable and easy to use, they accommodate originals of various sizes, and they provide acceptable image quality for a wide range of print publishing, multimedia, and OCR applications.

Until a year or two ago, color publishing professionals looked down upon the lowly flatbed, considering it suitable only for scanning *FPOs* (*for-position-only* artwork), which at press time would be replaced in the page layout by higher-resolution, higher-quality drum scans from the service bureau or color prepress house. Recently, however, flatbed scanners have become more versatile—capable of higher optical resolutions, higher color depths, broader dynamic ranges, and better support for multiple media formats. Price and performance considerations now make it more meaningful to distinguish among low-end, midrange, and advanced flatbeds than between flatbeds and other types of scanners. We'll survey the uses of flatbeds of all types, then examine the important differences between low-end, midrange, and high-end models based on optical resolution, color depth and dynamic range, media capabilities, imaging area, and case design considerations.

Low-End Flatbeds

For a few hundred dollars, you can buy into a flatbed scanner that will input reflective media (paper, hand-drawn artwork, photographic prints) for entry-level digitizing needs. Low-end flatbeds are useful for business communications, OCR, low-budget black-and-white or color print publishing, and input for media (such as presentations, multimedia, and video) where high resolution isn't critical.

The definition of "low-end" is a moving target. These days, even the lowest-end flatbed scanners offer at least 256-grayscale capability, and most can digitize in 24-bit color (although not without loss of detail in the shadow areas); some can even digitize transmissive media. Optical resolutions of 300 to 600 ppi are now the norm for this category.

Tip: The business communications uses of low-end flatbeds are also well served by a new class of multipurpose devices such as the PageOffice from UMAX. See the "Sheetfed and Multipurpose Scanners" section and Figure 3–12 for more about these.

Midrange Flatbeds

Thanks to a new generation of midrange scanners, communications and graphics professionals who routinely sent out for drum scans in the past can now do more of their print-quality scanning in-house. Midrange scanners fall in the $2,000 to $18,000 price range and are characterized by optical resolutions of 600 to 1,800 ppi, color depths of 10 to 12 bits per channel, improved dynamic ranges, larger imaging areas, and the ability to digitize slides, transparencies, and (in some cases) negatives as well as reflective originals—all features that make them more suitable for commercial-grade print publishing. Some of these scanners include software that permits on-the-fly enhancement of analog data based on the prescan, which avoids the quality loss that is inevitable with post-processing. Some midrange models even permit software-based batch scanning that lets you digitize multiple originals in one operation, perform separate prescan adjustments on each, and save each digitized image to a separate file. Figures 3–5 and 3–6 depict examples of popular midrange flatbeds.

> **❝Thanks to a new generation of midrange scanners, communications and graphics professionals can now do more of their scanning in-house.❞**

High-End Flatbeds

At the high end of the flatbed market (and with price tags of $35,000 to $50,000 to match) are units whose dynamic range, color depth, automated on-the-fly preprocessing, productivity enhancements, and hardware-based batch scanning capabilities compete with drum scanners. Like drum scanners, these models are best suited to work environments such as service bureaus, ad agencies, and magazine publishers, where high-volume scanning and quick turnaround are necessities. Figures 3–7 and 3–8 illustrate leading high-end flatbed scanners and their capabilities.

Under the Lid: Improvements in Flatbed Technology

Flatbed scanners have always been popular among graphic arts professionals because they're easy to work with mechanically: simply lift the lid, place the artwork on the glass (or Plexiglas) that separates it from the scan head, close the lid, and let the moving transport mechanism (aided by software) do the rest. Flatbeds in all price-performance ranges follow this basic ergonomic design, but differences among them impact the nature and quality of images they can digitize. Here's a brief look at the changes taking place under the lid that affect image quality and performance. If you're in the market for a flatbed scanner, it's helpful to investigate these nitty-gritty details when deciding among competing manufacturers' offerings.

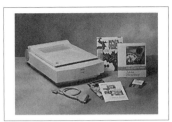

Figure 3–5   *Courtesy Epson America*

The Epson 1200C, with an optical resolution of 600 x 1200 ppi, samples color at 10 bits per channel. Dual connectors permit simultaneous use by Maintosh and PC systems. An optional transparency adapter allows scanning of transparent originals, and an automatic document feeder permits multiple-page scanning.

Figure 3–6   *Courtesy UMAX*

The Umax PowerLook, a 30-bit color scanner with a 3.0 density range, digitizes reflective or transmissive originals up to 8.3 x 11 inches in size using a maximum optical resolution of 600 x 1,200 ppi. Its MagicMatch color calibration software permits on-the-fly color and tonal adjustment and batch scanning.

Figure 3–7   *Courtesy Agfa Div. Bayer*

Agfa's 4,000-ppi SelectScan features 48-bit preprocessing, 39-bit A/D conversion, and a density range of 3.6. It handles both reflective and transmissive media up to 8.5 x 11 inches and supports batch scanning both through software and through a removable plate that can be mounted offline.

Figure 3–8   *Courtesy Scitex Corp.*

Scitex's Smart 730 scanner combines a flatbed device with a slave transparency scanner. It digitizes originals up to 11.8 x 17 inches in 36-bit color using a maximum resolution of 5,280 ppi and a dynamic range of 3.9. Productivity-boosting features include a robotic loader for batch scanning and artificial intelligence.

Optical Resolution

The number of sensor elements in a horizontal CCD array determines optical resolution. A few years ago, the size of the sensors limited the number that could be crammed into a desktop-sized scanner, but CCD designs are more compact these days. High-resolution CCDs increase a flatbed's effective enlargement factor, making it feasible to digitize small transmissive media (slides, negatives) and to enlarge small reflective originals many times.

Color Depth and Dynamic Range

Scanner manufacturers sometimes measure color depth in two ways. The *analog* color depth indicates how many raw light levels the CCDs can sense, noise and all; midrange and high-end flatbeds all claim bit depths at 30 to 36 (10 to 12 per color channel). These higher analog bit depths help ensure that at least 8 of the bits will be accurate in the saved image file, which brings us to the *processing* color depth—the number of bits left after the A/D converters sample down the analog voltages. The color depth standard among popular image editing software packages is 24 bits (8 per channel), but Adobe Photoshop supports limited use of higher-depth color information, and some sophisticated packages (Live Picture among them) permit full-featured use of high-bit color. A few of the midrange and high-end flatbeds can retain color information above 24 bits in the saved image file.

Keep in mind that higher bit depth doesn't automatically lead to a broader dynamic or tonal range. The signal-to-noise ratio of the CCD sensors used in a particular flatbed determine just how clean the color sampling is. CCDs come in many varieties, and the more expensive designs reduce noise interference through the use of additional silicon and better post-conditioning. A flatbed with a high signal-to-noise ratio and a 30-bit color depth might, in practice, reproduce better color than a device with a 36-bit color depth and higher degree of noise.

Tip: *As the color depth of an image increases, so does its file size. Plan for file storage space accordingly.*

> **❝***Higher bit depth doesn't automatically lead to a broader dynamic or tonal range unless the scanner also has a high signal-to-noise ratio.***❞**

The light source in a flatbed scanner also impacts the effective dynamic range. Newer-model and higher-priced flatbeds use either a cool fluorescent or tungsten halogen light source that reduces the generation of thermal heat. The reduced heat means that the scanning mechanism can be placed closer to originals and can expose them for a longer period of time to sample detail better.

Multiple-Media Capabilities

It used to be that flatbeds accepted only reflective media. Improvements in resolution and light source technologies now make it possible for the lowly flatbed to digitize slides, larger-format transparencies, and (in some cases) even negative film. In flatbeds, reflective artwork is lighted from below, while transmissive media are lighted from above, sometimes with the help of fiber optics located in the transparency adapter lid.

But although it's "doable" to scan transmissive media at 1,200 ppi, 1,200-ppi resolution may still be inadequate if you need to enlarge the really small originals (35mm slides, for example) more than a few times for print output. If you regularly digitize such small media and need high magnification factors, consider selecting a dedicated slide/transparency scanner, a high-end flatbed, or a desktop drum scanner for your shop—or sending out to have scans done at a service bureau.

The Drum Versus Flatbed Issue

There's a good deal of controversy in the industry about which type of scanner produces "superior" image quality: rotary drum scanners or flatbed scanners. All too often, these discussions miss the mark, since manufacturers and journalists tend to compare apples with oranges—desktop drum scanners with midrange flatbeds, for example. Drum scanning technology wins hands-down in such comparisons, because PMT sensing technology is capable of higher optical resolutions and produces a broader, cleaner dynamic range than the relatively inexpensive, noise-sensitive CCDs used in midrange flatbeds. A more equally matched comparison would be one between desktop drum scanners and the very highest-end flatbeds, where optical resolution, bit depth, dynamic range, productivity features, learning curve, and price tag are similar.

We feel that a better approach is to consider the issue from the standpoint of balancing technology with application and cost factors. If all you want to do in the kitchen is make toast, you don't need a fancy convex oven. On the other hand, if you're a gourmet chef aiming to attract well-heeled diners, you'd better outfit your establishment with something more high-powered than a microwave. Ask yourself questions like these to determine the best match between scanning devices and your needs:

- **How high a volume of scanning work do you handle?** If you need to batch scan, scan all day long, or run three shifts to handle your load, consider a desktop drum or high-end flatbed scanner equipped with artificial intelligence firmware and software. Midrange flatbeds will suffice for less demanding workloads.

- **What media do you usually digitize, and at what magnifications?** If you input primarily reflective or rigid originals that don't require many levels of magnification, flatbeds are your scanner of choice, hands down. If you handle slides exclusively, purchase a dedicated slide scanner and forget about the whole drum-flatbed conundrum. But if you digitize reflective and transmissive originals with equal frequency, you should probably use either a drum scanner or a dedicated flatbed plus a film/transparency scanner. That's doubly true if you scan many small-format originals that need high levels of magnification.

- **What are your typical end products, what audiences do they target, and how high is the budget?** If you're a commercial provider of scanning services (service bureau, print shop, design house, etc.), you need to know this information about your clients; if you're scanning for in-house use, then you need to know more about your own final output parameters. Take print publishing, for example. Only a limited range of tones can be reproduced in print even under optimum conditions. Characteristics of printing presses, paper stocks, and inks can limit tonal range even further. Drum scanning is therefore *de rigeur* for critical bigger-budget color and fine art publishing, where starting with the best tonal range possible is a necessity. But for commercial-grade printing or other types of output, midrange flatbed scanners may serve your needs adequately.

- **How critical are the issues of staff training and setup time for your organization?** Drum scanners require a steeper learning curve than flatbeds. Artwork preparation time is longer, and drum cleanup and maintenance are more extensive. If you have high staff turnover, limited staff skills, or no patience with mounting operations, you may experience greater satisfaction with the convenience of a flatbed.

Film and Transparency Scanners

For the graphic arts professional who needs to digitize *transmissive* media—35mm slides, film, or larger-format transparencies—only occasionally, midrange flatbed scanners with transparency adapters may suffice. But dedicated slide and film/transparency scanners have an important niche in the graphic arts input market, serving the higher-volume needs of color houses, newspapers, magazines, presenters, and marketing communications and MIS departments. The high optical resolutions of dedicated film/transparency scanners permit enlargement of small originals to sizes large enough to fill a magazine page or poster. And many dedicated film/transparency scanners include hardware- or software-based productivity functions. Imaging professionals who digitize both reflective and transmissive media regularly, but whose budgets don't permit the acquisition of a drum scanner, may find that a combination of a midrange flatbed and a dedicated film/transparency scanner meets their needs. Film/transparency scanners with a dynamic range of 3.0 or greater are also capable of producing high-quality scans that are barely distinguishable from those produced by drum scanners (see Figure C–2 in the color gallery).

With street prices ranging from just over $1,000 to more than $15,000, film/transparency scanners run the gamut of capabilities.Read on for a brief breakdown of what you can expect from scanners that digitize transmissive originals, and see Figures 3–9 through 3–11 for examples of leading low-end, midrange, and high-end film/transparency scanners and their feature sets.

Media Accepted

In the beginning there was the 35mm slide, the staple of many graphic arts professionals. Many lower-end and midrange film/transparency scanners such as the Agfa Vision 35, Microtek ScanMaker 35t, the Nikon Coolscan, and the Polaroid SprintScan 35, digitize only 35mm positives and negatives. Other midrange and high-end devices accept larger format transmissives, such as 6 × 7-cm, 2 $\frac{1}{4}$ × 2 $\frac{1}{4}$-inch, and 4 × 5-inch negatives and transparencies.

Figure 3–9   *Courtesy Scitex Corp.*

With a dynamic range of 3.7, Scitex's Leafscan 45 scans transmissives up to 60 × 70mm. Prescan correction is automatic.

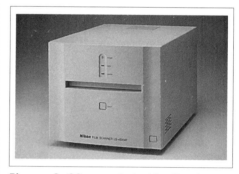

Figure 3–10   *Courtesy Nikon Electronic Imaging*

The midrange LS-4500AF from Nikon scans slides, transparencies, and film at 12 bits per color using resolutions of up to 3,000 ppi.

Figure 3–11   *Courtesy Polaroid Corporation*

The Polaroid SprintScan 35 speedily inputs 35mm transmissives at resolutions of up to 2,700 ppi. With a dynamic range of 3.0, it handles color correction automatically.

The Crosfield C360, Microtek ScanMaker 45t, PixelCraft Pro Imager 4520 RS, and Scitex Leafscan 45 are notable examples of multiple-media film/transparency scanners.

Tip: *Multiple-media capability doesn't necessarily go hand in hand with the highest resolutions. Before selecting a multiple-media scanner, make certain that its optical resolution is sufficient to digitize even the smallest 35mm media at the highest enlargement you'll need.*

Negatives are especially tricky to digitize because there's more to the process than just inverting color values from negative to positive. To digitize colors in negatives accurately, a scanner must compensate for two factors: the film itself (which creates a strong color cast) and the dyes in the film, which are based on the characteristics of color print stock rather than on the way the human eye perceives color. A few film/transparency scanners simply invert the color values of negatives, leaving the end user with the burden of performing color correction—not exactly a productivity-enhancing feature. Other manufacturers include *color look-up-tables* (called *LUTs* or *CLUTs*) for specific film types or provide hardware-based processing or software-based algorithms to smooth the negative-to-positive transition. If you're in the market to purchase a dedicated film/transparency scanner, inquire about negative color compensation features before committing to a particular model.

Optical Resolution

Optical resolutions for film/transparency scanners range from 2,000 ppi at the low end to the 5,083 ppi of the Leafscan 45. A 2,000 ppi resolution suffices for digitizing 35mm images that will be used in presentations and multimedia, and it can even reproduce images for commercial print publishing at sizes up to about 6 × 9 inches (assuming a line screen of 150 lpi). For

color print publishing requiring full-page images, however, you'll need at least 2,700- to 3,000-ppi capability, unless you're using originals larger than 35mm. Applications such as poster-sized print output of 35mm originals or long-term archiving of important corporate documents and databases require input resolutions of 4,000 ppi or higher.

Color Depth and Dynamic Range

Like their flatbed cousins, most dedicated film/transparency scanners use linear CCD arrays to sense color and gray levels and so are subject to noise and crosstalk. The more-expensive CCDs used in higher-end models have higher signal-to-noise ratios; midrange models use other compensatory techniques (brighter light sources, for example) to achieve cleaner color fidelity.

Dynamic or density range is even more critical for film/transparency scanners than for flatbeds, since densities are higher for negative, and especially positive films, than for reflective media. Dynamic ranges between 2.2 and 2.8, which define the low end of the film/transparency scanner spectrum, may not be able to capture all of the tones in slides and transparencies. Midrange devices feature densities at or a little above 3.0, and the high-end models boast dynamic ranges up to 3.7, which make them competitive with some desktop drum scanners.

Note: *Color slides and transparencies have an average density of 2.8 to 3.0. Higher densities are found only among duplicate slides and transparencies and those generated from special high-density films.*

The color depth spectrum for film/transparency scanners starts at 24 bits (8 bits per color channel) for the least expensive models.

Midrange devices typically sense 30 to 36 bits of color and optimize the tonal range for 24 bits. The highest-end models can sample 14 or even 16 bits of color per channel (42- or 48-bit color).

Productivity Features

Throughput is important for users of film/transparency scanners, or they wouldn't bother purchasing such a specialized device in the first place. Options vary but may include one or more of the following:

- **Adjustable focus**—Film/transparency scanners whose optics can automatically zoom in and out assure you of a more perfectly sharp scan by adjusting the focal length for different film sizes.

- **Built-in intelligence**—Some units include special processors to handle image preprocessing tasks (sharpening and/or color correction) quickly and automatically.

- **Batch scanning**—Midrange and higher-end units may include hardware-based batch scanning attachments and/or software accommodation for multiple scans.

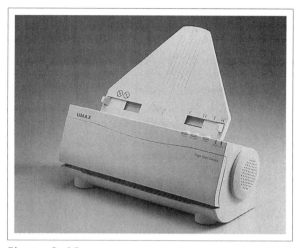

Figure 3–12   *courtesy UMAX*

UMAX's PageOffice 8-bit grayscale scanner comes with software that integrates OCR, fax scanning, e-mail, and electronic filing functions for the small office or home-based business.

include an automatic document feeder for scanning the multiple-page documents that clog any office. One example of the new multipurpose scanners is the UMAX PageOffice depicted in Figure 3–12.

Sheet-Fed and Multipurpose Scanners

For business communications such as OCR and archival, and for design shops where reflective artwork is used as a template for creating new originals, *sheet-fed scanners* still prove their worth. Sheet-fed scanners are usually black-and-white (1-bit) or grayscale (8-bit) and work by pulling a flexible original past a roller or other stationary mechanism. A new class of multipurpose business machines has recently arisen to meet the scanning needs typical in business communications such as OCR, e-mail, archiving, and fax. These often

Hand-Held Scanners

Hand-held scanners don't usually appeal to imaging professionals these days because their imaging areas, bit depths, and density ranges are extremely limited. The faster-better-cheaper trend among low-end flatbed scanners has also tended to crowd hand-held devices out of the market. However, hand scanners do have a niche among PC users, primarily in the fields of business communications (OCR) and low-end or in-house desktop publishing. These compact devices are also useful for scanning small reflective originals or surfaces of cumbersome items (bulky books, carpet patterns, furniture covers, etc.) that don't easily fit onto the platen of a flatbed.

Filmless Cameras

Filmless cameras—digital cameras, still video cameras, and video capture boards—are challenging scanners' monopoly over the means of capturing images for input into the computer. These devices actually have very different uses. Whereas still video cameras and video capture boards digitize images primarily for use in multimedia and video, digital cameras are coming into their own in print publishing applications of all kinds. Let's take a brief survey of these rapidly developing types of "scanners."

Digital Cameras

Filmless photography sounds like a great idea—an end to toxic chemicals, processing time, scanning, and second-generation–quality originals—but its practical implementation has taken many years to develop. In a digital camera, the visual recording element is not film but one or more linear or rectangular CCD arrays. The number of pixels that record discrete units of visual information is directly linked to the number of cells or photodiodes in the CCD—and therein lies a stumbling block. The crop of digital cameras available just a few years ago could image only a few hundred thousand pixels per shot, compared with the up-to-20-million–pixel resolution that fine-grain slide film in an analog 35mm camera represents. Images captured with these low-resolution cameras are acceptable when viewed on a monitor or television but (with the exception of small newspaper photos) are too grainy for print media.

Recently, however, the industry has made great technological strides in many directions—in color depth, in imaging speed, in the amount of information that can be captured per shot, and in image storage options that help free the camera from the computer and make it as suitable for live action shots as for

Electronic Versus Film-Based Image Capture

If you have a background in traditional photography, you may find the lingo surrounding the new medium of digital cameras a bit overwhelming at times. Rest assured, though, that there are strong correspondences between the terminologies of the old and new ways of capturing images. For example:

- **Resolution**—The electronic term "resolution" has a direct relationship to the notion of grain size in silver-based films. A high-resolution digital camera is comparable to fine grain in a film.

- **Equivalent ISO ratings**—Unlike scanners, digital cameras measure dynamic range in terms of equivalent ISO (International Standards Organization) ratings rather than density. This has to do with the digital camera's roots in traditional photography, where film speeds determine the light sensitivity of a film. There's a direct correspondence in terms of dynamic range, contrast, and grain size between the ISO ratings used for digital cameras and the ASA ratings used for traditional cameras. Lower ISO ratings translate to lower-contrast images with high resolution and a broader tonal range, while higher ISO ratings indicate higher-contrast images with lower image resolution and a narrower tonal range.

catalog or studio work. Today's digital cameras fall into three general categories, each of which has its own market niche:

- Low-resolution cameras that have limited internal memory or storage units, permitting the camera to take several shots with no direct connection whatever to a host computer. These cameras, of which the Apple QuickTake 150 in Figure 3–13 is a notable example, produce output suitable for use in multimedia, video, newspapers, and (provided the images are printed at small sizes) collateral print media such as newsletters and catalogs.

- Midrange cameras, which use CCD arrays large enough to generate image files that contain several megabytes of information, typically have color depths greater than 24 bits, and their CCDs feature a strong signal-to-noise ratio. Some of these cameras, such as the Crosfield Celsis 130 and 160 (Figure 3–14), must be connected directly to a computer, which renders them useful for product photo catalog work or studio fashion photography but too awkward to handle in spontaneous situations. Newer-model midrange cameras, such as the Nikon E2s (see Figure 3–15), can save images to high-capacity removable storage media or to flash memory cards, both of which liberate them from the computer and pave the way toward use in live action shots. Keep your eyes on the midrange cameras; they're the most exciting area to watch in terms of near-future commercial development.

- At the high end of the digital camera market are *scanning cameras* whose extremely high resolutions and color depths require up to several minutes) per multimegabyte capture. The Dicomed Digital Camera Back (Figure 3–16)

Figure 3–13   *courtesy Apple Computer*

The Apple QuickTake 150 camera, for use on either the Macintosh or Windows platform, takes snapshots at a resolution of 640 x 480 pixels and can store 16 high-quality or 32 standard-quality images on an internal memory card. It includes a snap-on close-up lens for capturing images at short distances.

Figure 3–14   *courtesy DuPont Crosfield*

*The Crosfield Celsis 160 (**top**) captures images at 1/12 or 1/500 of a second and generates file sizes of up to 3.5MB. The Celsis 130 (**bottom**) is a studio camera with an ISO equivalent rating of 80. It captures images at five different resolutions with capture times ranging from 3 to 16 seconds and generates file sizes of up to 21MB.*

Figure 3–15   *courtesy Nikon*

The Nikon single-lens reflex E2s can record up to seven continuous pictures at three frames per second and at a resolution of 1,280 x 1,000 pixels. The camera, which has an ISO equivalent rating of 800 to 1,600, saves JPEG-compressed images to a high-speed removable storage card with a 15MB capacity (43 images).

Figure 3–16   *courtesy Dicomed*

The Dicomed Digital Camera attaches to the back of existing 4 x 5-inch view cameras. Featuring a 6,000 x 7,520-pixel resolution and equivalent ISO ratings of 50 to 200, its long capture times (2 to 13 minutes) and large file-size output (up to 130MB) require that it be tethered to a desktop or portable computer during shooting.

is an example of such a camera, which must be connected to a host computer and is therefore best suited to medical, scientific, still-life, catalog, and time-lapse photography.

As you can see from the foregoing examples, there's still an inherent tradeoff between the optical resolution of a digital camera and its portability and speed of image capture, which in turn impact the camera's suitability for still life or action shooting. Look for that tradeoff to dissipate gradually after the example of the Nikon ES series and the Kodak 460, as larger removable storage devices gain currency and as new CCD designs and optics permit faster imaging. If you're considering using a digital camera as a primary digitizing device, find out as much as you can about each model's resolution, portability, color depth, equivalent ISO rating, lighting requirements, and image storage options.

Tip: *Like flatbed and transparency scanners, digital cameras vary in their susceptibility to noise. A primary cause of noise is temperature variance among individual CCD elements. The proprietary Fuji-based chip technology used in the Nikon ES series cameras compensates for this variance, resulting in an exceptionally low level of noise and correspondingly high image integrity. Investigate and compare signal-to-noise ratios when considering the purchase of a digital camera.*

Still Video Cameras and Video Capture Boards

Video images, whether transmitted through still video cameras or video capture boards, contain an analog signal suitable for viewing on a television. One consequence is that capturing a full frame of information requires two passes. This *interlacing* of data makes video-captured images good candidates for output to computer-based presentations, but poor candidates for print out-

put or interactive multimedia, where visual artifacts or apparent fuzziness may manifest. To remove such artifacts, apply a de-interlacing filter such as the one available in Adobe Photoshop.

Dynamic range can also be an important consideration when you're using video-generated images. Remember the tradeoff between CCD sensor size and light sensitivity that we mentioned in Chapter 2? The size of individual CCD sensors in video cameras is very small, so still video cameras require more ambient light than film-based cameras in order to capture adequate detail and dynamic range. In addition, still video cameras produce images within a *video-legal* color range that is narrower and more saturated than the CMYK gamut used in print media. Performing tonal adjustment, color correction, and color balancing in an image editing program is a good idea when you're planning to use video-generated images in other output media.

An additional factor to consider when working with video-generated images is the amount of information available and its implications for output size. Still video cameras limit their capture area to what will fit on a television screen—a mere 512 × 480, 640 × 480, or (at the most) 756 × 576 pixels in the USA, Canada, and Japan, where *NTSC* (National Television Standards Committee) resolution is the norm. At best, images of this size would print well only in product catalogs, real estate flyers, in-house newsletters, or other media where images remain small or resolution is less important than content. Some video cameras interpolate images to far higher resolutions.

Photo CD Images

Our focus in this book is on skills for those who need or want to do their own scanning. These days, though, obtaining images on Photo CD is becoming as popular as doing it yourself.

When photos are distributed on those little gold disks, it's all too easy for imaging professionals to forget that Photo CD images are scanned images, too. As such, they are subject to the same kinds of quality criteria as images that are digitized by other methods. If you use your Photo CD images for real-world projects (and why else would you get them?), you should understand how the images arrive on the CD-ROM in the first place and how the method of digitizing them affects their suitability to your chosen output medium.

> ❝ *It's all too easy for imaging professionals to forget that Photo CD images are scanned images, too.* ❞

Photo CD Basics

Eastman Kodak originally envisioned Photo CD as a mass market product that consumers could use to view their photographs on a television or computer monitor. But Photo CD has found its true following among photographers, publishers, graphic designers, and other communications professionals who have found Photo CD a way to obtain "ready-made" electronic images at low cost. In response, Kodak has developed new formats for distributing Photo CD images to meet the needs of these users.

You can obtain Photo CD images in several ways. Many stock photography houses now routinely distribute their stock catalogs in Photo CD–compatible format, and some online image database services do the same. To have your own (or a supplier's) photographs

recorded onto CD-ROM, you simply send your slides or film to a photofinishing lab or service bureau equipped with a Kodak Photo CD Imaging Workstation (PIW). The CD-ROM that you receive from any of these sources can be read by both Macintosh and PC-compatible computers equipped with a CD-ROM drive. (Multisession drives are required only when you have additional images recorded onto a CD-ROM at a later date than the original set.)

Whatever your imaging application, you owe it to the success of your projects to be familiar with the factors that impact Photo CD image quality. Some of these factors— the equipment used to digitize the images, the proprietary Photo CD format, color encoding, and compression standards—are controlled by the photofinishing lab or service provider. The end user has control over the software used to download the finished images and the image resolution.

Photo CD Color Encoding and Compression

Photo CD image data is recorded using a proprietary, device-independent color system known as *YCC*. The theory behind the YCC color space is that the human eye perceives color primarily according to *luminance* or brightness and only secondarily according to *chrominance* or hue. In the YCC color system, each pixel has three color values: the *Y* value represents luminance and the two *CC* values represent the position of the color on a theoretical hue-saturation axis. (You can learn more about YCC and other perceptual color spaces in Chapter 5.)

The YCC color space is intricately linked with the compression that Photo CD images undergo. This compression process in turn has some effect on image quality, as the following look at Master Photo CD processing demonstrates.

Behind the Scenes at a Master Photo CD Imaging Workstation

At the Photo CD workstation (see the "Photo CD Imaging Workstations" section following), an original undergoes several processing steps. First, it is scanned at the maximum size possible for the processing format requested (Master, Pro, etc.) and encoded according to the YCC color space. Next, the image data is compressed several times. During the first compression, approximately 75 percent of the data in the two *CC* channels is thrown away, yet this barely changes the perceptible color characteristics of the image because most of the luminance (*Y* channel) information is retained. In the second compression, software algorithms perform color averaging on the data that remains in the two chroma channels; the resulting file is then decompressed and compared to the largest size original, and the difference between the two versions, called a *residual*, is stored. When the end user later opens the image at the largest available size, this residual information is retrieved. The Kodak software algorithms repeat this process of averaging, decompressing, and comparing again, producing the *Base* version of the file and a second residual. The two smallest image resolutions are generated by downsampling from the Base version. Finally, the workstation operator records to disk the five image resolutions that make up the proprietary *Image Pac* for the Master Photo CD format. Pro Photo CD images are available at an even higher sixth resolution. Table 3–1 provides a handy reference to the various Image Pac resolutions and their dimensions, file sizes, and recommended output sizes for print publishing applications. Refer to Chapter 7 for more information about resolution as it relates to printing.

When an end user opens the image at the highest resolution, *both* of the residuals created during the compression process are integrated into the decompressed file to minimize color degradation. Opening the image at

Image Resolution	Colormap Size (pixels)	File Size (K, MB)	Maximum Recommended Enlargement (Assumes 1.5:1 screen-frequency-to-resolution ratio)			
			85 lpi	133 lpi	150 lpi	200 lpi
Base/16	128 × 192	72K	1.0" × 1.5"	0.64" × 0.96"	0.57" × 0.85"	0.42" × 0.64"
Base/4	256 × 384	288K	2.0" × 3.0"	1.28" × 1.93"	1.14" × 1.71"	0.85" × 1.28"
Base	512 × 768	1.1MB	4.0" × 6.0"	2.57" × 3.85"	2.28" × 3.41"	1.71" × 2.56"
4 Base	1,024 × 1,536	4.5MB	8.0" x 12.0"	5.13" × 7.7"	4.55" x 6.83"	3.41" x 5.12"
16 Base	2,048 × 3,072	18MB or 24MB (Print Photo CD)	16" × 24"	10.26" × 15.4"	9.1" × 13.65"	6.83" × 10.24"
64 Base	4,096 × 6,144	72MB or 96MB (Print Photo CD)	32" × 48"	20.53" × 30.8"	18.20" × 13.65"	13.65" × 20.48"

Table 3–1

Photo CD Images: Colormap Size, File Size, and Recommended Print Dimensions at Selected Halftone Screen Settings

the second-largest resolution integrates only the second residual with the file. Images encoded using the Print Photo CD format are available in uncompressed high-resolution versions for the most demanding color publishing applications.

Service Provider Color Balancing Options

Although the equipment and software used in Photo CD workstations is standardized, Photo CD service providers can exercise some judgment options that affect the color characteristics of the recorded image. They can enhance the preview image before scanning it, and they can optionally compensate for the color characteristics of a specific film emulsion.

> **"***Photo CD service providers can exercise some judgment options that affect the color characteristics of the recorded image.***"**

Prescanning image enhancement

PIW operators can compensate for under or overexposure of the source images or adjust the overall color balance of the preview image before scanning (see Chapters 6 and 8). Both mass-market and custom Photo CD service providers apply these types of adjustments automatically to negative films. Custom photofinishers and service bureaus, who tend to cater to imaging professionals, can also enhance slide and transparencies on a case-by-case basis using the preview that appears on their monitor. If you require custom enhancement, use the services of such a supplier.

Compensating for film emulsion characteristics

Negative films and unmounted slides and transparencies display the film manufacturer, film type, and speed along the outer edge of the medium. At the time of processing, Photo CD service providers must choose between *scene balance*—standardizing color representation across film types to eliminate color casts—or retaining a specific film emulsion's unique color characteristics. In cases like the following, scene balance is *not* desirable:

■ When photographs are taken under controlled artificial lighting, as in studio work

■ When a specific film is used to emphasize color and tonal qualities unique to that film (many professional photographers are particular about this)

Whenever you want the Photo CD image to faithfully reproduce the color and tonal qualities of the original without special compensation, instruct the service provider to apply a *universal film term* in *lock beam mode*. These settings automatically disable scene balance and achieve film-consistent color without subjective judgments on the part of the operator. Figure C–3 in the color gallery shows examples of how Photo CD color reproduction differs according to whether the operator turns scene balance on or off.

Photo CD Formats

Five different types of Photo CD image formats are currently available: Master Photo CD, Pro Photo CD, Print Photo CD, Catalog Photo CD, and Portfolio Photo CD. Each format is useful for a different set of imaging applications.

Master Photo CD

Master Photo CD is the original Photo CD consumer format. Only 35mm negatives and slides can be accepted for this type of processing, which can encode up to 100 Image Pacs on a single CD. Master Photo CD images come in five different resolutions: 16 Base, 4 Base, Base, Base/4, and Base/16. As you might guess from Table 3–1, the 16 Base and 4 Base versions are most suitable for commercial-grade print publishing, while the Base version is better suited to video or multimedia output or small-format printing in catalogs. The two lowest-resolution versions are generally too small to use as anything but reference images.

Pro Photo CD

The Pro Photo CD format was developed with the needs of professional photographers (and, to a more limited extent, print publishing professionals) in mind. Larger-format films (120mm and 4 × 5-inch), as well as 35mm films, are accepted for processing. Image Pacs include the five resolutions of the Master Photo CD format, plus an optional sixth, higher resolution called 64 Base (see Table 3–1). With a resolution of 4,096 × 6,144 pixels, 64 Base images occupy 72MB of space; so depending on the film format, between 25 and 100 Pro Photo CD Image Pacs can fit on a disc. Another Pro-specific feature is the ability to enter caption and credit information for each image.

Print Photo CD

Of special interest to ad agencies and other high-end print publishing professionals is the Print Photo CD format, which was developed to store color separations and finished page layouts, as well as photographic images. Artwork is stored at an *uncompressed* 64 Base resolution, and images are scanned by high-end drum scanners from companies such as Dupont Crosfield, Linotype-Hell, and Scitex. End users can request either YCC or CMYK color encoding for their images.

Catalog Photo CD

Catalogs tend to include many images printed at small sizes. Catalog publishers and print professionals who need images only as FPO placeholders will appreciate the Catalog Photo CD format, which provides up to 4,500 images per disc in small formats. Only the three lowest-resolution versions of the Image Pac—Base, Base/4, and Base/16—are available.

Portfolio Photo CD

Created for presentation professionals and multimedia developers, Portfolio Photo CDs can store up to 800 images along with sounds and other graphics. The accompanying software allows the end user to create interactive presentations using buttons and scripts. Through a special agreement between Kodak and Kinko copy centers, end users can author their own CD-ROMs using Portfolio Photo CD at selected Kinko's stores throughout the U.S.

Photo CD Imaging Workstations

The proprietary Photo CD Imaging Workstations (PIWs) used to generate Photo CDs are complete systems that include all the hardware and software to carry out the processes of scanning, preview and enhancement, color encoding, CD recording, and thumbnail printing. Expensive and designed for high-volume throughput, they are typically found only at selected photofinishing labs and some service bureaus and color houses. Several configurations of PIWs are in use depending on the format selected for processing. For example, the Kodak PIW 2400 workstation (Figure 3–17) is geared toward serving the needs of both consumer and commercial customers ordering images in Master Photo CD format. It includes a flatbed scanner with an automatic film loader for batch scanning film (density range 2.8), a UNIX-based Sun

Figure 3–17 *courtesy Eastman Kodak*

The Kodak PIW 2400 workstation digitizes 35mm film and transparencies and encodes the images in Master Photo CD format.

Figure 3–18 *courtesy Eastman Kodak*

The Kodak PIW 4200 workstation can handle 35mm and larger-format transmissives for encoding onto Pro Photo CD format.

Sparc workstation as the data manager, two Kodak Photo CD disc writers, proprietary software for adjusting, color encoding, and recording images, and a color printer for printing the thumbnail images that appear on the Photo CD jacket. For Pro Photo CD customers, the PIW 4200 workstation (Figure 3–18) substitutes a film/transparency scanner that can sample both 35mm and larger-format films. This scanner is capable of sampling at 36-bit color depth. Scanners used for both Master and Pro Photo CD processing have a density range of 2.8, which is adequate to capture the entire tonal range of many commercially available negative films. Print Photo CD workstations utilize industry-standard high-end drum scanners that can capture the entire tonal range of even the densest transparencies.

Obviously, both the type of original (film negative, slide, or transparency) and the processing format impact the quality of the final images you receive on CD. If you request Master Photo CD processing for negatives, the workstation will be able to capture all the detail in the originals because the density range of the scanners used for Master Photo CD processing equals or exceeds that of negative films. Transparencies, on the other hand, can have a density higher than 2.8, so 35mm slides recorded in Master Photo CD format may not contain the full range of tones of the original. For print publishing professionals, a good rule of thumb is to request Pro Photo CD processing for slides and transparencies when artwork is to be used in commercial-grade documents, and to request Print Photo CD processing when artwork is destined for high-budget, color-critical printing applications. If you obtain stock photos in Photo CD format, be sure to ask the provider about the medium of the original images and the format used for encoding them.

Accessing Photo CD Images

As an end user, you can exercise some control over the quality of the images you download from a Photo CD. Assuming you're planning to use Photo CD images for print publishing, you should do the following to achieve the best results:

- Access the images using software that gives you the greatest control over color and tone.
- Choose the correct resolution for your application.
- Sharpen the image.

Maintaining Color Integrity During Access

Images recorded using the Print Photo CD system are available in both Photo YCC and CMYK TIFF formats so no conversions between disparate color gamuts are necessary.

With Master Photo CD and Pro Photo CD images, however, a conversion must take place from YCC to some other color space, typically RGB or CMYK. This conversion is complicated by the fact that YCC images are stored with color depths of 12 bits per channel, whereas most image editing packages support only 8 bits per channel for editing. Picking the correct gamma for conversion from YCC to RGB is critical, as it determines *which* range of the 12-bit tones you actually utilize. How can you optimize the dynamic range of the image as it's downloaded to your computer?

Caution: *Beware of assuming that the availability of Print Photo CD images in CMYK TIFF means that the color gamut is already optimized for print media. Each printing discipline (sheet-fed, heat-set web, or newspaper) requires a separate color separation setup, and each requires a unique undercolor removal (UCR) or gray component replacement (GCR) setting to compensate for dot gain. One size of CMYK TIFF doesn't fit all!*

Tip: *Future versions of Adobe Photoshop will support and write to the Kodak Image Pac format.*

Many Photo CD access modules exist, from Kodak's stand-alone Photo CD Access Plus to high-end plug-ins such as Purup's PhotoImpress. But if you use industry-standard editing packages such as Photoshop, Fractal Design Painter, PhotoStyler, or Picture Publisher, your best option for accessing Photo CD images is to use Kodak's KPCMS (Kodak Precision Color Management System). On the Macintosh, KPCMS installs as a System Extension when you install Photoshop; various configurations are available for other software packages and platforms. By selecting "File: Open" in Photoshop, the dialog box shown in Figure 3–19 will be displayed.

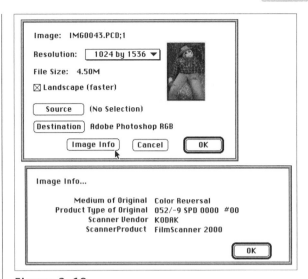

Figure 3–19

Information about the original medium and scanning parameters for a Photo CD image can be obtained by accessing the Kodak KPCMS dialog box and then selecting the Image Info button

Tip: *In Photoshop, choose LAB as the color mode to guarantee the most accurate conversion of color data. LAB color, like YCC color, describes color in terms of luminance and chrominance and is device independent. If you have to convert the Photo CD image to another color mode (such as CMYK) later in the image editing process, you won't suffer any loss if you start out with LAB. That's not the case if you bounce back and forth between RGB and CMYK.*

The goal of KPCMS is to ensure consistent, predictable color by calibrating image color display on a monitor to both the image source (in this case, Photo CD) and the destination output device (monitor or print setup). Kodak supplies several source and destination color profiles, called *precision color transforms*, with the basic KPCMS module; other modules are available directly from Kodak. Figure 3–20 shows the dialog boxes in which you choose the desired source and destination transforms.

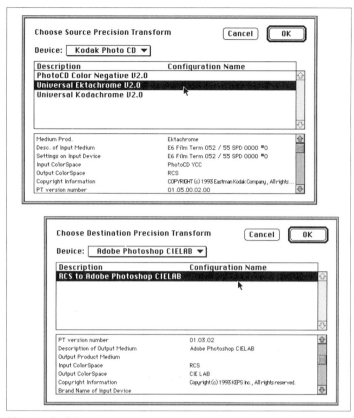

Figure 3–20

*Selecting a source (**top**) and a destination output device (**bottom**) when downloading Photo CD images helps ensure consistent color for your chosen method of output.*

Choosing the Best Resolution

Your second responsibility when downloading Photo CD images is to select the highest-resolution version that your application is likely to require. Base images are adequate for images that will be used in computer-based media, but higher resolutions may be necessary for print publishing projects. See Table 3–1 and refer to Chapter 7 for information on how to determine image resolution for print output.

Sharpening Photo CD Images

Photo CD images are not sharpened by the service provider, so for print publishing applications, some sharpening is required after you have resized the image to its final output size. An unsharp masking type of filter generally yields better results than a sharpening filter or tool. For more information about sharpening images that have already been digitized, see Chapter 8 and *Preparing Digital Images for Print* (Berkeley, CA: Osborne/McGraw-Hill, 1995), also in the Osborne/McGraw-Hill Digital Pro Series.

Stock Photos on CD-ROM

The number of vendors providing stock images on CD-ROM is increasing almost daily. Each provider has its own rules and regulations for negotiating rights. In some cases, you buy rights to use the images outright when you purchase the CD, but in others, you need to negotiate fees for one-time use based on the commercial value and circulation you expect for your project. Although many vendors supply images in Photo CD format, others provide them as CMYK TIFF files or in a proprietary file format. If quality is a primary concern, you may want to inquire about the equipment and processing used to digitize the stock images and encode them onto CD-ROM.

We've devoted this chapter to a survey of input sources available to imaging professionals. Once you've chosen an input device or have gained a better understanding of the device you're already using, it's time to review your computer system and ensure that it's properly set up for scanning. Onward to Chapter 4!

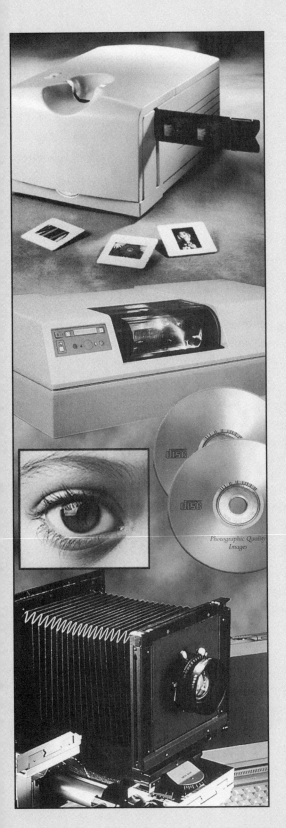

4

Setting Up a Professional Scanning System

There's more to a successful scanning experience than simply having the right kind of scanning equipment and skills at your disposal. Smooth communication between the scanning device and the hardware and software components of the host system is equally important. If the host system is too slow, lacks the necessary RAM, runs out of image storage space, or has a small or flickering monitor, frustrating bottlenecks can occur. If your system's display adapter can't show all the colors in the images you scan, or if you neglect to calibrate input, display, and output devices, you risk introducing errors into the scanning and image editing processes. And if you're not aware of important scanning-related software, you could be missing out on opportunities to increase productivity and improve accuracy.

This chapter makes recommendations for setting up a professional scanning system, always with a view to the types of scanning you do most. Obviously, what constitutes a "professional"

43

system depends on your projects; independent designers, quick-print shops, service bureau prepress operators, advertising or marketing communications professionals, and production staff at a book or magazine publishing house have widely varying requirements. Do you scan color, grayscale, or black-and-white originals? Do your file sizes tend to be large or small? Will your primary output be to in-house printers, imagesetters, computer monitors, or video? And how many scans do you need to produce every week or month? Answer these questions, and you can then determine whether your scanning "kitchen" requires a gourmet food processor, a blender or mixer, or simply a sturdy wooden spoon. For a quick overview of system setup recommendations based on typical scanning requirements, see Table 4–1.

Processing and Bus Speeds

The adage "You never can have a fast enough computer or too much memory" rarely rings more true than when it applies to scanning and processing raster images. Whatever your scanning requirements and volume, it seems that your existing system never can quite catch up to the greed for speed. That's especially the case if you scan color originals. Color, considered a luxury just a few years ago, is now becoming almost *de rigeur* for imaging and design professionals; a recent industry survey by *Publishing & Production Executive* magazine found that nearly 85 percent of print publishing–related businesses now do at least some color scanning in-house. Color images generate file sizes that are three or four times the size of comparable grayscales (see Chapter 5), and it takes a lot of processing power to wield those multi-megabyte files.

> **❝*You never can have a fast enough computer or too much memory for scanning and processing raster images.*❞**

Although the *central processing unit* (*CPU*) of a computer isn't the only determinant of a system's speed, it's a major factor. As Table 4–1 suggests, professionals involved in low-end scanning applications may find that a Macintosh Quadra (based on the Motorola 040 series chip) or a 486-based PC meets their needs. Macintosh users involved in midrange color scanning projects may be able to get by with higher-speed 68040-based Macs but should probably look to PowerPC systems, which are based on Motorola's *RISC* or *reduced instruction set* chips. RISC-based chips achieve high speeds by repeatedly building complex instructions out of simpler core instructions. Windows scanning professionals should perform their tasks on Intel Pentium-based machines or, at the very least, 486-based PCs having clock speeds of 66 MHz or above. The Pentium and newer PowerPC machines have the added advantage of being built around a *PCI* (*Peripheral Component Interconnect*) bus, whose 64-bit data highway for the management of all processing operations greatly improves throughput over older machines based on a 32-bit data highway. At the high end of the imaging market, throughput requirements dictate the use of a high-speed PowerPC, Pentium, or UNIX-based workstation from companies such as Sun Computer Systems or Silicon Graphics. High-end workstations running under the Macintosh operating system are also becoming available—witness the DayStar Genesis MP depicted in Figure 4–1.

	Scanning Requirements	Processor Speed	RAM	Monitor	Display	Image Storage	Imaging Software	Misc.
Low end	Grayscale reflective originals File sizes < 1MB Print output, small dimensions Presentations, 640 x 480 monitor < 10 scans/week	Mac: 040 or later PC: 486 or above	8MB or greater	14- or 17-inch	256 or more colors	Hard drive >500MB Floppy disk Removable hard drives	Photoshop (Mac/PC) Picture Publisher (PC)	Modem, 9600 baud or faster
Midrange	Color reflective and transmissive originals File sizes > 4MB Print output, medium to large dimensions Multimedia, presentations, video output 10 to 30 scans/week	Mac: 040 or Power PC PC: 486/50 or Pentium	16 to 64MB	19- or 21-inch	24-bit color	Hard drive > 1GB Removable hard drives Magneto-optical drives (128MB or 230MB)	ScanPrepPro or Photoshop-compatible plug-ins Photoshop (Mac/PC) Picture Publisher (PC) Proprietary high-end scanner packages Image database software	Modem, 14,400 baud or faster Color management software Drawing tablet
High end	Color, mostly transmissive, some reflective originals File sizes > 10MB Print output, medium to large dimensions >30 scans/week	Mac: PowerPC or Mac workstation or dedicated Photoshop accelerator PC: Pentium UNIX-based workstation	> 64MB	21-inch	24-bit color, accelerated	Hard drive >2GB Array drives Removable hard drives Magneto-optical drives Writable CDs	Photoshop (Mac/PC) Live Picture (Mac/UNIX) ScanPrepPro or Photoshop-compatible plug-ins Proprietary high-end scanner packages Image database software	Modem, 14,400 or 28,800 baud Color management software Drawing tablet Hardware calibration devices

Table 4–1

Recommended System Setups Based on Typical Scanning Requirements

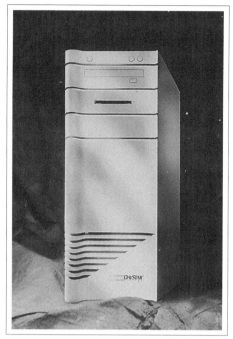

Figure 4–1   *Courtesy DayStar Digital*

The DayStar Genesis MP, a high-end workstation running under the Macintosh operating system, features dual upgradable 120 MHz PowerPC processors for multiprocessing of complex tasks.

If you or your company needs to upgrade to meet scanning demands but can't afford to chuck your entire investment in an older machine, alternative upgrade paths are available. Macintosh users, for example, can upgrade their logic board directly through Apple Computer or through a clone manufacturer, or purchase third-party accelerator boards. Each approach has its advantages. If you obtain a new logic board, you will gain extra speed because you are upgrading the bus as well as the CPU. On the other hand, you may have to invest in new RAM because the new logic board doesn't accept your existing memory chips. If you buy a third-party CPU accelerator, you can retain your existing RAM memory but may experience less than a maximum increase in speed because your bus and memory speeds are slower than those in a newer computer.

Windows users seeking to upgrade their equipment can obtain inexpensive motherboard replacements through clone manufacturers. The motherboards of many existing PCs include upgradable CPU chips, which the user can simply replace with one that doubles the clock speed.

RAM

For scanning and image processing tasks, having sufficient *RAM (random access memory)* is even more vital to system performance than having a fast CPU and bus. To run smoothly, many leading image editing packages require an amount of RAM equal to three to five times the file size of the image you're currently working with (Photoshop uses five times the amount of image data in a file). HSC Live Picture, which uses RAM only to shuttle screen-sized proxies of the full image, still requires a minimum of 24MB, with 48MB recommended. That's above and beyond the amount of RAM needed to run your operating system (Macintosh or Windows) and any other software you may have open at the same time! If an image editing program requests more RAM than you have available, it typically uses a scheme called *virtual memory*, which dips into your hard drive and uses its free space as pseudo RAM. Even the fastest hard drive is slower than RAM, so having to resort to virtual memory noticeably slows your performance. You're better off investing in extra memory for the sake of throughput.

Monitors and Display Adapters

The monitor and display adapter that make up your display system can also present bottlenecks to scanning quality and performance. Monitor size and image definition, resolution, dot pitch, color depth, and the speed of screen redraw are all equally important for the scanning professional.

Monitor Size, Monitor Resolution, Display Resolution, and Dot Pitch

Seeing is what it's all about, right? Throughput and accuracy in scanning demand that you be able to view as much of a digitized image at a 1:1 viewing ratio as possible. Constantly scrolling and mousing around to verify the results of prescan gamma, color balancing, or unsharp masking settings wastes your time unnecessarily. Matching the monitor size, monitor resolution, display resolution, and dot pitch to your scanning applications assures you of the most accurate viewing possible.

Even seasoned imaging professionals sometimes confuse monitor resolution with display resolution. *Monitor resolution* measures the number of pixels that can be displayed horizontally and vertically on a screen at one time—1024 × 768, for example. *Display resolution*, on the other hand, is expressed in dots per inch (dpi) and measures the density of the information on the screen. On the Macintosh platform, where monitor size and display resolution are standardized to match one another, you can count on viewing an image at a WYSIWYG 72 dpi (one point per pixel) when image viewing magnification is set to 1:1. On the Windows platform, 1:1 viewing is a little trickier; standards are looser and display resolution is denser, often ranging from 80 dpi to over 100 dpi. Whichever platform you work on, it's still advantageous to be able to view as much of an image at a glance as possible.

If you routinely scan only small grayscale originals, or if you input low-resolution color images that are intended for either multimedia output or print output at small sizes, a 17-inch monitor with a maximum monitor resolution

of 1024 × 768 pixels may meet your needs (see Table 4–1). But for scanning larger-format color images, a 19- to 21-inch monitor and even higher display resolutions are in order. Also pay heed to the *dot pitch* of your monitor, which affects the crispness and definition of the pixels you see. For scanning and imaging applications, 17-inch monitors should have a dot pitch of .26mm or lower, and larger monitors should feature a dot pitch of .28mm or lower.

Color Depth and Display Acceleration

Matching the color depth of your display adapter to the color depth of scanned images is vital to ensure color fidelity during pre- and postscanning processing (see Chapter 5). If you scan in 24-bit color (16 million colors) but can view no more than 32,000 colors on your monitor, you could be missing important details that hamper the accuracy of scanning and editing judgments you make. Trouble is, there's an inherent trade-off between the number of colors that can be displayed at a given resolution and the amount of time and memory required to redraw all the pixels on the screen: the higher the bit depth, the slower the screen redraw. To counteract this problem and improve screen refresh rates, many manufacturers offer display adapters that have multiple megabytes of memory on-board, or that include DSP (digital signal processor) chips and software specifically to accelerate Photoshop performance.

Note: *To save on on-board memory, some 24-bit display adapter manufacturers reduce the number of colors that can be viewed at higher resolutions. Choose an adapter that displays 24-bit color at the highest monitor resolution you will use.*

Image Storage and Transfer Solutions

Over 90 percent of respondents to a survey by *Publishing & Production Executive* magazine affirmed that their image storage needs are increasing. And no wonder! The use of color scans is growing; presentations are going digital; thousands of multimedia frames need to be archived somewhere; and companies, ad agencies, and publishers are handling an increasing share of their large-format color scanning in-house.

With the number of image files and their sizes both increasing, floppy disks are passé as a viable storage medium, even with compression (see Chapter 9). Many options are open to the imaging professional; let your choice be guided by such factors as typical file size, number of files to be stored, and ease of exchange with clients, service bureaus, or vendors.

Internal Hard Drives

Properly speaking, internal hard drives aren't long-term storage devices. Consider them as work drives—short-term storage solutions where scanned images can park only until the project's over. Even for short-term storage, though, hard drive speed and capacity requirements are increasing as images continue to get bigger, hungrier, and more numerous.

When evaluating a hard drive for speed, look especially carefully at the rated seek time, access time, and transfer rate. *Seek time* measures how quickly the drive head can travel to the physical location on the track from which it will read or to which it will write data. *Access time* is the amount of time needed for the drive data head to begin reading or writing data from within the track. *Transfer rate* refers to the amount of data that can pass back and forth between the computer and the hard drive in

one second. High-capacity drives boast both the shortest seek times and the fastest transfer rates; some 2GB drives, for example, may feature a seek time of less than 8 ms (milliseconds) and a transfer rate of 4 or 5MB per second.

If you or your networked colleagues regularly scan and manipulate images with file sizes of 20MB or greater, however, then even these speeds may retard your progress. Consider a *disk array*, also known as a *RAID drive*. In a disk array setup, two or more separate high-speed drives are connected through a SCSI controller and appear as a single drive volume to your system. The controller shuttles data between the two drives as you work; while one disk is writing a block of data, the other disk is available for the next block. In this way, disk arrays optimize read/write times—often achieving transfer rates of 7 to 12MB per second, two or three times the maximum rate possible with a single disk. Disk arrays, available from APS, FWB, and other manufacturers, are especially useful for networked multiuser imaging and high-volume production environments (see the Image Storage column of Table 4–1). Figure 4–2 shows a Sledgehammer II disk array configuration from FWB.

Removable Drives

Removable magnetic hard drives have long been a standard for data backup and for transferring data to and from service bureaus, clients, publishers, and designers. They're convenient to use and the drive mechanisms are easily affordable, even for low-end scanning professionals. Originally, removable drives were available in low capacities only—44MB for SyQuest cartridges or 10 to 20MB for Bernoulli drives. As image storage needs have grown, so have removable drive capacities. On the PC side, tiny, removable PCMCIA drive cartridges are gaining in popularity as backup options for both laptops and desktop systems. Figure 4–3 depicts a high-capacity 270MB removable drive subsystem from SyQuest.

For all their convenience, removable drive cartridges have some disadvantages. They're magnetic and are more susceptible to damage and data loss than are optical cartridges. The lower-capacity drives are also much slower than hard drives, making them more suitable for archival than for current work. Finally, although the cost of drive mechanisms is low, the per-megabyte storage cost of the removable cartridges themselves is higher than for opticals.

Optical Drives

Rewritable magneto- and phase-change optical systems and rewritable CDs are fast emerging as the new standards for high-volume, portable storage. Their popularity as alternatives to removable magnetic drives is due to their higher capacities, greater data reliability, and low per-megabyte storage cost. The cost of optical drive subsystems is higher than for magnetic removable drives, but if you have truly high-volume image storage needs, the low cost of the optical cartridges will soon offset the expense of the hardware.

Rewritable optical drives come in one of three basic types: magneto-optical, phase-change optical, and rewritable CD systems. Multiple-drive jukeboxes are also commercially available for network servers.

Magneto-Optical Drives

In magneto-optical (MO) drives, a laser writes to a removable 5.25-inch or 3.5-inch plastic or glass cartridge by rapidly heating and cooling the disc so that it becomes charged magnetically. Outside magnetic influences can't influence the media and data at room temperature, so data stored on MO is extremely stable.

MO drives are available in capacities of 128MB, 230MB, 600MB, 650MB, 1.3GB, 2.0GB, and 2.6GB. Drives with capacities below 660MB are best suited for backup and archival, since their access times and transfer rates are too low for use as work drives. However, higher-capacity 1.3, 2.0, and 2.6GB drives *can* be used for current projects, as their transfer speeds approach those of fast hard drives. Many service bureaus, prepress houses, and full-service printers support 128MB, 230MB, and 650MB MO media for data exchange (see Figure 4–4).

Figure 4–2   *Courtesy FWB*

FWB's Sledgehammer II 4GB disk array for Macintosh AV and PowerMac systems achieves a seek time of 4.0 ms and a sustained transfer rate of 13.5MB per second.

Figure 4–3   *Courtesy SyQuest Intl.*

A SyQuest 270MB-capacity removable drive system and cartridge

Phase-Change Optical Drives

Phase-change technology differs from MO technology in that it doesn't use any form of magnetism in either the drive or the disc media. This allows the laser in the drive head to write or erase in one pass as opposed to three, changing the normally amorphous material of the disk to a crystalline state and back again. Phase-change drives, typically available in a 5.25-inch, 1.5GB

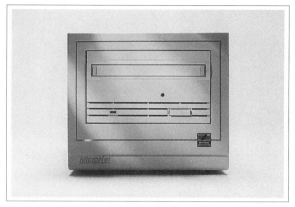

Figure 4–4   *Courtesy MicroNet*

The 1.3GB-capacity MicroNet SB-TMO-1300 MO drive features an access time of 18 ms and a sustained transfer rate of 2MB per second.

Figure 4–5   *Courtesy Pinnacle Micro*

Pinnacle Micro's RCD-1000 offers a recordable CD system, a double-speed CD-ROM reader, and optical storage in a single drive.

configuration, offer about 15 percent additional storage capacity per disc when compared with MO drives.

Multifunction Rewritable CD-ROM Drives

Also based on phase-change technology, the new multifunction opticals combine a double-speed or quad-speed CD-ROM reader with writable CD and optical storage functions. The media for these drives can store up to 650MB of data, making them ideal for multimedia and Photo CD development, as well as backup and data transfer—and its versatility reduces equipment clutter on your desktop. Rewritable CD media are also inexpensive, offering 650MB capacity at less than $15 per disc. See Figure 4–5 for an example of a rewritable CD-ROM drive.

Tape and DAT Tape

Tape drives and *DAT* (*digital audio tape*) drives remain popular, economical backup choices for single-user systems and networked servers, respectively. DAT drives can accommodate 2 to 10GB of storage per tape cartridge, which translates to just pennies per megabyte.

But although tape backup may be cheap, it's not quite as data reliable as some other types of mass storage. Tapes can break, data transfer speeds are too slow to permit use as a work drive, and backup software must act as an intermediary to make file transfer possible. For moderate- to high-volume scanning applications, tape is also inconvenient. As files in a project change, you have to update the tape contents incrementally, saving the newest files in a separate volume rather than keeping all current project files together. And if you want to erase any old or outdated files on a tape, you must erase the entire tape. Removable drives and opticals have no such limitations. For long-term storage and archival, tape proves its usefulness; but for critical scanning and imaging tasks, turn to other mass storage media.

File Compression Solutions

No matter what storage media you choose, there may still come a time when you run out of space. File compression comes to the rescue. To take a closer look at compression standards and their implications for scanned images, refer to Chapter 9.

Modems

Although not a storage technology per se, modems are essential for scanning professionals and service vendors who must exchange image files. For image file transfer (and for transfer of PostScript versions of image files), speed is of the essence; you should be equipped with the fastest modem you can afford. Currently, the fastest modem standard is 28,800 baud (bits per second), and a baud rate of 14,400 is the absolute minimum you should consider.

Since modems are digital, while telephone lines are analog devices, modem speed alone won't guarantee an optimum transfer rate between your business and the other end of the line if telephone line noise gets in the way. Many telephone companies now offer a special noise-free telephone connection, called an ISDN connection, for a monthly fee. ISDN assures high-speed, digital-quality telecommunications. If your projects have high-volume modem transfer needs, it may be cost effective to establish an ISDN connection.

An Imaging Software Arsenal

An entire industry has grown up around raster images and scanning. A veritable arsenal of software now exists to guide you through every imaginable step in handling images, from scanning to editing, from image management to output. Here, we provide a brief overview of the most essential types of software.

Scanning Software or Plug-Ins

Most high-end scanning devices come equipped with proprietary stand-alone scanning software, while midrange and lower-end devices typically supply Photoshop-compatible plug-ins.

Among plug-ins, the range and quality of tasks and processing operations vary widely. If the scanning software for your device doesn't prepare an image for output to your complete satisfaction, you'll need to perform *post-processing* in an image-editing or image-processing package to bring the artwork up to snuff.

Image Database Software

As the number of images per project continues to grow, so does the need to organize them. Image cataloguing software provides several useful functions in this regard. Use it to group images into projects, issues, chapters, or other organizational units; keep track of updates; provide thumbnail printouts for a quick overview; and include annotations for each image in the project. Among the most popular cross-platform image database packages are Adobe Fetch and Kudo Image Browser (Figures 4–6 and 4–7). Kodak Shoebox is a popular choice for managing Photo CD images exclusively.

Calibration and Color Management Products

No matter how expensive a scanning system you assemble, it won't produce high-quality results unless each hardware device in the production chain—scanner, monitor, proofing printer, and so forth—can match the color or grayscale tones in the original accurately. The term *calibration* describes the process of adjusting a device to a given standard so that its tonal reproduction remains constant over time. On a higher level, calibration also refers to the process of matching the color characteristics of multiple hardware devices to one another so that the color of images passed between them remains consistent.

Higher-end drum, film/transparency, and flatbed scanners calibrate themselves internally every time you turn them on. Midrange flatbed

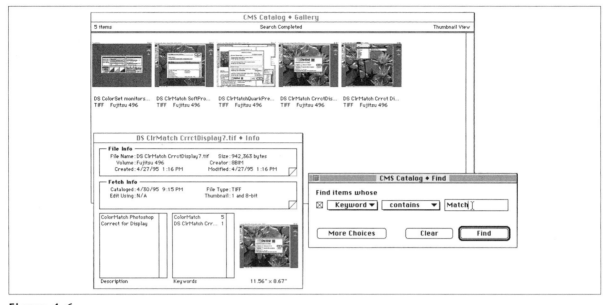

Figure 4–6

Adobe Fetch offers comprehensive tools for cataloguing, annotating, and updating large numbers of images in a project.

and film/transparency scanners use another approach. Many desktop scanners ship with calibration software and an industry standard grayscale or color *reference target* on film or reflective media. You calibrate the scanner by scanning the target and allowing the accompanying software to measure your unit's color reproduction characteristics against the manufacturer's standard for that product. The calibration software records any deviation from that standard as a custom *profile*, which you can apply to images after scanning to compensate. Figure C–4 in the color gallery shows several industry standard reference targets. Many standard image-editing packages also include calibration tools for those users who lack other means to calibrate their scanners.

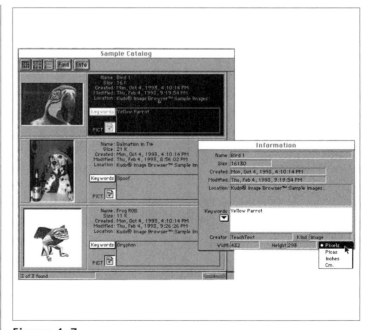

Figure 4–7

Kudo Image Browser is another full-featured image database package for managing large numbers of images.

The scanner is only one device in the color reproduction chain, however. The monitors, proofing devices, imagesetters, film recorders, and printing presses you use for your scanning projects also need to be calibrated to one another to avoid image degradation. For more information about this larger theme of *color management*—standardizing color reproduction across devices—see Chapter 5.

Image Editing Software

This category encompasses everything you can possibly do to an image between scanning and output. A majority of imaging users on Macintosh, Windows, and UNIX-based systems have adopted Adobe Photoshop as a standard. Its color correction, compositing, and production-related tools and native special-effects filter set make it a comprehensive solution for both production and creative professionals. Other outstanding image-editing packages on the Macintosh are HSC Live Picture and Fauve XRes, which define new standards of speed in image handling. Under Windows, Micrografx Picture Publisher is one of the original pioneers in developing sophisticated layering and color-enhancement functions.

Getting Painterly

For those who scan mainly to obtain an image that can serve as a basis for creative manipulation, Fractal Design Painter offers enormous creative options on both the Macintosh and PC platforms. Fauve Matisse

caters to a similar market for Windows-only imaging users. Adobe Photoshop's open architecture filter standard also has helped to spawn a burgeoning aftermarket in special-effects filters. Among the most well-known filter sets are Adobe Gallery Effects, Andromeda's Series I, II, and III (see Figure 4–8), Cytopia's PhotoLab, Kai's Power Tools from HSC Software, and Xaos Tools Paint Alchemy.

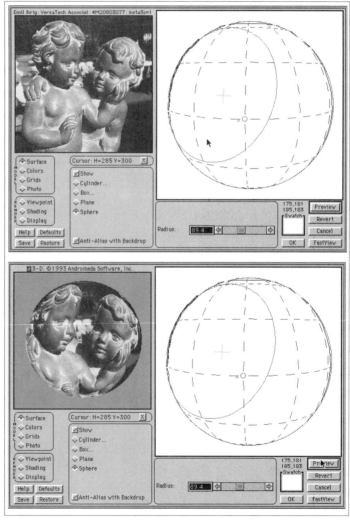

Figure 4–8

*Andromeda's Series 2 3D Surface Mapping filter in action. **Top:** An original image being prepared for 3-D filtering. **Bottom:** Previewing a 3-D sphere rendering within the Andromeda dialog box*

Getting Productive

Many separate processes go into preparing an image for output. The busier the imaging work environment, the greater the need for software that can automate complicated, multiple-step procedures. Two especially noteworthy plug-ins that automate image processing for print publishing applications are ScanPrepPro from ImageXpress, Inc. and IntellihancePro from DPA Software. Both products use artificial intelligence to optimize each image. Intellihance Pro (Figure 4–9) lets you calibrate scanner input; create custom print output profiles; and define and save settings for optimizing grayscale, RGB, or CMYK images. ScanPrepPro (Figure 4–10) is built around an extensive lithographic database gleaned from the developer's three decades in the printing industry. It handles every conceivable image-processing function—tonal and color adjustment, descreening and sharpening, dot gain and moiré compensation, resizing and resolution adjustment, and color separations—according to user-definable settings. ScanPrepPro can adjust a scanner's input settings automatically in the background.

Other image-automation software is geared toward batch processing without reference to specific output media. DayStar Digital's freeware PhotoMatic plug-in for the Macintosh (Figure 4–11) helps automate processing through customizable scripting. Equilibrium DeBabelizer also provides scripting functions geared specifically to images destined for multimedia output.

Regardless of your output goals, a firm grasp of color basics is essential to assuring high output quality. That's the subject we'll take up in the next chapter.

Figure 4–9

Intellihance Pro uses artificial intelligence to tackle image processing tasks.

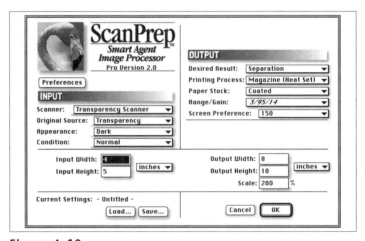

Figure 4–10

ScanPrepPro offers intelligent scanner setup and automated postprocessing for scanned images.

Figure 4–11

DayStar PhotoMatic permits batch processing of images in Photoshop through user-customizable scripting.

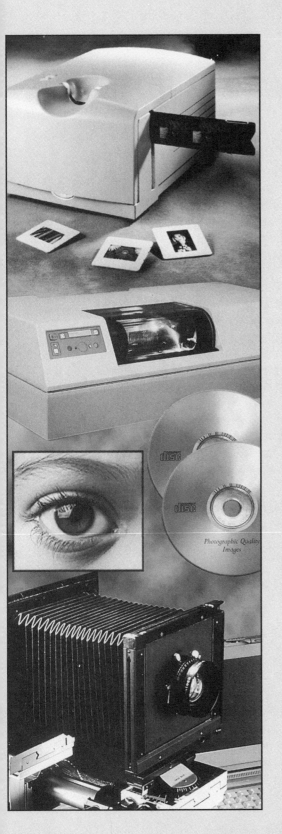

Photographic Quality
Images

5

Color Fundamentals for Scanning

Well over 80 percent of businesses involved in print communications now do at least some color scanning in-house.
That percentage—which doesn't even take into account
any of the scanning done for multimedia, presentations, video, or
business communications output—is likely to continue growing as
tools for handling color become increasingly powerful, affordable,
and user friendly. Innovations in scanning technology are making
improved tonal ranges available to a broader spectrum of end
users; image-editing packages are offering enhancements in speed
and color-output sophistication; color printing is becoming less
expensive; and new standards for describing color are spawning a
host of color management products designed to streamline the
process of ensuring color consistency.

Even with the accessibility of all the new color tools, you'll get
better results from scanning if you have a broad acquaintance with
color fundamentals. In this chapter, we'll provide basic information

about how color is described digitally; the relationships between bit depth, number of color channels, and file size; techniques for calibrating scanners, monitors, and output devices; and how color management software and hardware devices can help standardize color as you transfer images between devices.

To create first-class color output, print publishing professionals should also acquaint themselves with halftoning basics and image-editing techniques for eliminating moiré and minimizing dot gain. We'll cover some of these issues in Chapters 7 and 8.

Defining Color

Apples are red, the sky is blue, and grass is green. But there are many varieties of apples, the shade of the sky changes according to the time of day, and grass may lean toward brown or yellow depending on how dry the weather is and what species of grass you're dealing with. Even in "analog" nature, there's tremendous variation among everyday colors that we take for granted. There's also the issue of communicating color. When you tell someone else about an apple, a sky, or grass that you've seen, there's no guarantee that the picture he or she has in mind will match, even remotely, the color you saw.

This simple example shows how complex the task of describing color in precise, universal terms can be. That's the goal to which color scientists have committed themselves. Without universal "languages" of color, without a way to define color in standardized, numerical terms, scanning, image editing, and digital output would be unthinkable.

Color spaces, also called *color models*, are the means by which science describes color in conceptual and quantifiable terms. A basic grasp of the conceptual representation of color allows you to understand the relationships between colors and makes it much easier to select colors

by number using a standard color picker in your favorite image-editing package (see Figure 5–1). Over the years, multiple color spaces have been developed to meet the needs of various industries or groups in describing how light is transmitted, absorbed, or reflected by specific media. Artists and designers, for example, traditionally have used the HLS or HSB color space; computer industry professionals describe color in RGB terms; and the CMYK color space is the standard in the commercial printing industry.

Whatever its basis, every color space must satisfy three requirements. It must specify color in a standardized, *device-independent* way that doesn't rely on the capabilities of any single transitory device. It must also delineate the *gamut*, or range, of the colors it describes. Finally, it must account for the way in which the perception, transmission, or reflection of light determines that gamut. For these reasons, we can break down color spaces into three groups: *perceptual*, *additive*, and *subtractive*. Figures C–5 through C–8 in the color gallery illustrate how color science represents these three types of color spaces visually.

Perceptual Color Spaces

In the design and communications industries, the ultimate reference for color is the human eye. Our eyes can perceive only a small fraction of existing electromagnetic wavelengths; but even so, the visible spectrum comprises billions of colors—far more than any scanner, monitor, printer, or television can reproduce.

The perceptual color spaces used most widely today are variants on the one first developed in the 1920s by the CIE (Commission Internationale de l'Eclairage). The three-dimensional CIE color space (see Figure C–5 in the color gallery) describes any perceptible color in terms of values on a three-dimensional axis. One value describes *luminance* (the brightness component of a color, which itself has no hue) while the other two

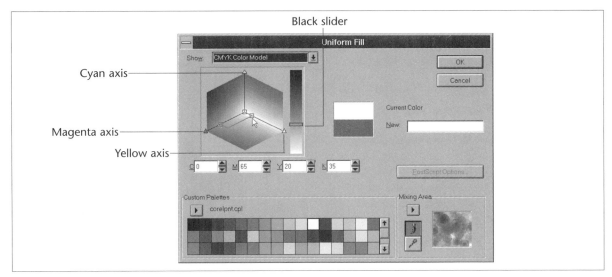

Figure 5–1

The color selection dialog boxes in Corel PhotoPaint! use a visual representation of color models to help users specify colors numerically.

relate to actual *chroma* or color values. CIE color's comprehensiveness and device independence are the foundation for some of the technology behind color management software, Photo CD, and Adobe Photoshop. Kodak's proprietary YCC color scheme used for Photo CD images and the LAB color space used by Adobe Photoshop both have their roots in CIE color, which makes it possible to transfer images between devices and modes without color degradation.

Although CIE color encompasses the entire visible spectrum, it's not intuitive to use in terms of specifying color numerically. Perceptual color spaces with which artists and designers are more familiar are HLS (hue, lightness, saturation) and HSB (hue, saturation, brightness). In these systems, you can describe any color using three values that represent *hue*, *lightness* or *brightness*, and *saturation*. Software color pickers express hue in terms of degrees, and express lightness or brightness and saturation (the intensity of a color) values in terms of percentages. Color scientists visualize the HLS and HSB color spaces as a six-sided cone in which hue corresponds to a color's position in a circular rainbow color wheel, saturation to its position relative to the perimeter or interior of a cone, and lightness or brightness to a color's position along the vertical axis of the cone (black at the bottom to white at the top).

Additive Color Spaces

The RGB color space is the natural color "language" of scanners, computer and television monitors, and other electronic devices, which reproduce color by *transmitting* light rather than reflecting or absorbing it (see Figure C–9 in the color gallery). The color you see on computer monitors, for example, comes about when electron beams strike red, green, and blue phosphors coating the screen, causing them to emit light in varying combinations—up to 256 for each of the three primary colors (16.7 million total). In much the same way, the red-, green-, or blue-coated CCD elements in scanners and digital cameras emit voltages when light strikes them.

> *"The RGB color space is the natural color language of scanners, computer and television monitors, and other electronic devices."*

We call the RGB model an *additive* color space because colors are generated by adding colored light to colored light. Secondary colors are therefore always brighter than the red, green, and/or blue primaries that combine to create them. Adding maximum intensities of red, green, and blue produces white in the RGB color space (see Figure C–6 in the color gallery). Combining equal values of red, green, and blue produces neutral shades of gray, with low values producing darker grays and high values producing lighter ones.

Sixteen million colors may seem like an infinite number, but as Figure C–5 in the color gallery shows, RGB color has a much narrower gamut than the visible spectrum. Even so, the color gamut that monitors can display is sufficient for photorealistic editing.

Subtractive Color Spaces

Figure C–7 in the color gallery demonstrates that if you subtract one of the primary RGB colors from white light, you obtain colors complementary to red, green, and blue. Green and blue with red subtracted produce cyan; red and blue with green subtracted produce magenta; and red and green with blue subtracted produce yellow. Surprise! You have CMY, three of the four components in the CMYK color space that is the basis for color mixing in the printing industry.

In a *subtractive* color space like CMYK, mixing two or more primaries generates additional colors by *absorbing* some light waves and

reflecting others. Cyan ink, for example, absorbs red light and reflects green and blue; magenta ink absorbs green light and reflects red and blue; and yellow ink absorbs blue light and reflects red and green. Figure C–8 in the color gallery shows the principles of subtractive color mixing at work. Whereas in the additive RGB model light is added to light, producing brighter colors, in the subtractive CMYK model light is subtracted, producing darker colors. This inherent difference between computer display technology and the pigments in printers' inks explains why the colors in an image that looks brilliant on your monitor appear darker and duller when they are printed. If your image-editing package allows it, preview images in CMYK as you work in RGB mode to accurately forecast and correct for the CMYK color gamut.

The RGB and CMYK color spaces are complementary to one another, at least in theory. But there's a gap between theory and practice. Mixing maximum intensities of cyan, magenta, and yellow should produce black (the complement of white, which is produced by mixing red, green, and blue), but on press they yield a dirty brown due to impurities in pigment properties and a deliberate imbalance toward cyan that occurs when RGB is converted to CMYK. That's where black comes in. Black is the *key color* (K) that printers add to cyan, magenta, and yellow to produce deeper, richer blacks and shadow tones with better definition.

Of course, the addition of a fourth color skews the conversion equation, making it somewhat more complex to juggle color correspondences between RGB and CMYK. There's no simple one-to-one correspondence anyway; the CIE color representation in Figure C–5 shows that although the RGB and CMYK color gamuts overlap, they don't match exactly. If you use Adobe Photoshop, you can prove this for yourself simply by selecting a particularly bright or saturated RGB color in the Color Picker dialog box, as shown in Figure 5–2. The appearance of the

Desired color | Gamut warning indicator

Closest substitute

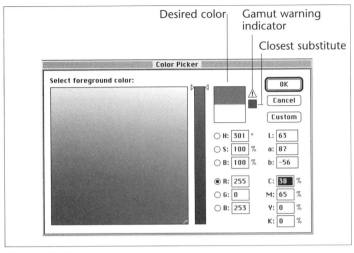

Gamut warning inactive

Figure 5–2

Photoshop's Gamut Warning indicator in the RGB Color Picker indicates that a particular RGB color is outside of the CMYK gamut and represents how the closest printable substitute will look.

exclamation mark inside the triangle signals that the chosen RGB color simply can't be reproduced using process color inks. Try activating Photoshop's Gamut Warning command on a particularly brilliantly colored RGB image (Figure 5–3) to find out just how much of it is unprintable without modifying color and tonal range!

Color Depth, Channels, and File Size

Most scanning devices permit you to choose from among several different scanning *modes*: line art (black and white), grayscale, indexed color, 24-bit or higher-bit RGB color, or CMYK. Scanning modes define the bit depth or color depth of the sampling, which in turn has a direct relationship to the file size of the scanned image. Figure C–1 in the color gallery shows the relative file sizes for an original scanned at each bit depth.

- *Bitmap* or *line art* mode (1-bit) reproduces all the tones in the original artwork as either black or white. Each pixel contains only one bit of information, so file sizes are

Gamut warning active

Figure 5–3
© Emil Ihrig

When Photoshop's Gamut Warning command is active, the program masks out all the colors in an image that are impossible to print using CMYK inks.

compact. Scan OCR material at a maximum of 300 ppi, but scan line art at a very high input resolution—up to the resolution of the final printing device or 1,200 ppi, whichever is lower (see Chapter 7).

- *Grayscale* mode (8-bit) reproduces all the tones and colors in the original using 256 shades of gray. Each pixel contains eight bits of information, so files are eight times as large as for comparably sized originals scanned in line art mode.

- *Indexed color* mode (also 8-bit) reproduces the image using a palette of 256 colors. The resulting file size is approximately the same as for scanning in grayscale mode. Few scanners provide an indexed color mode option, but most major image-editing packages let you convert from 24-bit RGB color to indexed color.

- *24-bit RGB color* mode (24-bit) reproduces an original at 8 bits (256 colors) per channel, producing file sizes that are 24 times as large as a comparable bitmap and 3 times as large as a grayscale.

- *High-bit RGB color* mode (available for only a few higher-end scanners) records the digitized original at 12 to 16 bits per channel (4,096 or 65,536 colors per channel, respectively), producing files that are 36 to 48 times as large as a comparable bitmap and 4.5 to 6 times as large as a grayscale.

Note: *Most scanners that sample images at 10 to 16 bits per channel actually record only 8 bits per channel in the final digital file.*

- *CMYK color* mode (32-bit) reproduces images using four color channels at 8 bits per channel. File size for CMYK-scanned images is one-third larger than for RGB-scanned images. Scanners that save to CMYK actually scan in RGB, then create color separations.

In the near future, you also can expect to see more products that permit scanning into six or seven color channels—for example, two sets of RGB, CMYK plus RGB, CMYK plus CMY, or CMYK plus metallic colors. This multiple-channel, *hi-fi color* approach to scanning has as its goal the achievement of more saturated printed colors than are possible with four-plate CMYK separations.

To Scan or Not to Scan in CMYK

High-end and desktop drum scanners give you the option of immediately converting RGB-scanned images into the CMYK color mode (see Figure C–10 in the color gallery). This option may look attractive if you plan eventually to output color images to print, but it's not always advantageous. You'll benefit from direct CMYK mode scanning only if these conditions apply:

- You simply plan to place the scan into a page layout and don't need to retouch or edit the image.

- You or the scanning service provider already knows which press type, paper stock, and printing inks will be used for the job and how they will impact dot gain, desired tonal range, black ink generation, and color balance.

- You use an image-editing package that permits editing in CMYK mode *and* your system has lots of RAM memory to handle the larger file sizes.

It's usually not practical to scan in CMYK if you must extensively retouch or creatively embellish on a scanned image. The color characteristics of the image may change substantially during the editing process, so that it's not worth the trouble to clog up memory and hard drive space with the 33 percent larger file size of a CMYK scan. Instead, scan and edit the image in RGB, and when it's time for output, translate the file first to CIELAB color (which contains both the CMYK and the RGB gamuts) and then to CMYK. The same holds true if you won't be assigning paper stocks and press types until well on in the project. CMYK separations will not be accurate if you create them before you have a firm grasp of all press conditions.

Calibration

Perhaps you remember a game called "Gossip" from your childhood. A group of kids sits in a circle, and the first child whispers a sentence into the next child's ear. That child immediately has to repeat the sentence into the ear of the neighboring kid. By the time the garbled message travels all the way around the circle and back to the ears of its originator, it bears little or no resemblance to what was actually said and provides amusement for everyone. All too often, the color print publishing "game" plays itself out in a similar way—but no one laughs, because the "message" is color, and the players have invested money, careers, and reputations in it.

Matching color is a constant concern for print communications professionals and is important for those working in other media as well. The task of making a final printed, recorded, or videotaped image look like the undigitized original encounters many obstacles. Potential obstacles include the inherent differences in gamut between RGB and CMYK color; variations in the way scanners, monitors, proofing printers, and imagesetters interpret color; and the tendency of even a single piece of equipment to reproduce color inconsistently over time. The crucial issue becomes a question of how to standardize color representation along every link in the input-to-output chain.

Calibration provides part of the solution. Calibration is a two-step process. The first step involves adjusting a single piece of equipment (such as a scanner) to match a standard for consistent color representation. It's important frequently to calibrate each input and output device in your system—scanner, monitor, printer, film recorder, and so on—using an industry-standard color target. You then must take the essential second step of matching the color characteristics of all the devices in the production process to each other. That's the

tricky part. Not only does each type of device reproduce color according to a different standard, but variations also exist among multiple manufacturers' implementation of the "same" product. Calibration can't do the job alone; it needs help in the area of *describing* the color representation characteristics of any device in a standardized way.

To meet that need, a type of software product called a *color management system* (abbreviated as *CMS*) has arisen. The object of a CMS is to achieve color consistency throughout the production workflow by describing and recording the color reproduction characteristics of various devices and models in a universal, device-independent way, and then using the recorded information to translate the color characteristics of any one device to any other. Although no CMS solution is perfect (see the "Color Management Solutions" section of this chapter), they are an invaluable aid to standardizing color.

> **❝ The object of a CMS is to achieve color consistency throughout the production workflow. ❞**

The Calibration Process

The ideal calibration process for scanning professionals involves several steps. It's important to begin by standardizing your *color environment*—the lighting and colors in the area where you work. Other steps include calibrating your scanner, monitor, and output devices individually, printing a color proof, and adjusting devices to compensate for any color inconsistencies noted.

Standardizing the Color Environment

Many factors, from subjective emotions to external lighting conditions, influence how the human eye perceives color. We can't account for emotions, of course, but it *is* possible to control many of the objective factors in the environment where you work. Observe these guidelines to ensure that your environment is as free from distracting variables as possible:

- Scan and view images in an area where lighting doesn't change much over the course of the day (and night, if you work at night). If your work area has windows, use blinds or shades to keep lighting uniformly dim, and avoid placing the workstation where it's subject to glare. If the room has no windows, use a lighting source that provides even, consistent, and subdued illumination in a neutral color.

- Make sure that the wall coloring in your work area is neutral, subdued, and uniform.

- Bright colors surrounding images can distort your perception of the image colors, so set the background color of your monitor to a neutral gray. On the Macintosh, use the General control panel (for System 7.1 or earlier) or the Desktop Patterns Control Panel (for System 7.5 or later) to do this. Under Windows, use the Color dialog box for version 3.11 or earlier, and the Monitors control panel in Windows 95.

Calibrating Monitors

Having established a consistent color environment, the next step is to calibrate the monitor on which you view scanned images. An uncalibrated monitor can introduce apparent color casts into images, which may not faithfully represent the contents of the digital files. Most monitor calibration tools work by aligning display colors back to the manufacturer's specifications.

For best results, calibrate a monitor only after it has been running for at least half an hour to ensure that its colors have stabilized. It's also important to calibrate frequently (monthly if you're using software-based calibration), since the phosphors in a monitor change with age.

There are three basic types of tools for calibrating monitors: software utilities that ship with image-editing packages, hardware-based calibrators, and the monitor profiles that are part of color management systems. The volume of scanning work that you process and the image-editing package you use will dictate which of the three approaches best serves your needs.

Caution: *Avoid using more than one type of monitor calibration tool simultaneously. Each utility or device can skew the results of any others. If you work with multiple image-editing packages, use a third-party color management system or hardware calibration device.*

Image-editing calibration utilities

Most image-editing packages include a software utility for calibrating monitor display. Some utilities offer only basic options, such as adjusting the representation of grays and colors to eliminate color casts. Others can even compensate for the chromaticity values of the red, green, and blue phosphors produced by a specific brand of monitor. The Gamma utility (Figure 5–4), developed by Knoll Software and shipped with Adobe Photoshop, is a particularly comprehensive example of a software utility. The Gamma utility allows you to adjust many monitor display parameters, including

- The neutral, linear representation of gray shades

- The monitor's white and black points (the brightest and darkest shades that the monitor can display)

- The *gamma curve* of the monitor, which adjusts a monitor's ability to distribute tones evenly between its white and black points
- Color balance, through direct manipulation of red, green, and blue phosphor emissions

The Gamma utility also allows you to save and load multiple calibration settings for various purposes, such as variable lighting conditions or matching a monitor's display characteristics to paper stocks for separate projects.

Hardware calibration devices

Service bureaus, ad agencies, and other environments with high-volume scanning needs may find a hardware calibration device more convenient to use than a software utility. Hardware calibration devices—typically consisting of a suction-cup sensor that attaches to the monitor, plus accompanying calibration software—match viewing conditions on a monitor to the lighting conditions under which final output will be viewed. Graphic arts professionals traditionally measure these conditions in terms of Kelvin temperature. Without calibration, most monitors have a white color temperature between 6,300 and 9,300 degrees Kelvin. But the standard for viewing color print work is 5,000 degrees Kelvin, equivalent to the color of white seen under bright sunlight at noon. Hardware calibration devices adjust the monitor's white point to the desired Kelvin temperature, which automatically adjusts all the other colors that the monitor can display. They also allow you to calibrate the monitor's gamma curve and color balance.

Hardware calibration devices work well with color management systems, because they can save digital profiles of a monitor's characteristics to disk. Depending on how the device's software specifies this information, one or more color management software packages may be able to read the profile and use it to help calibrate the entire input/output cycle. Radius' SuperMatch Display Calibrator, for example, writes monitor profiles that are compatible with Kodak/DayStar Digital's ColorMatch, Agfa's FotoTune, Apple's ColorSync, and EfiColor Works. The DayStar Colorimeter 24 pictured in Figure 5–5 feeds monitor profile information into the Kodak/DayStar ColorMatch system.

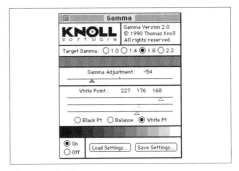

Figure 5–4
Knoll Software's Gamma utility provided with Photoshop (here in its Macintosh version)

Figure 5–5   *Courtesy DayStar Digital*
The DayStar Digital Colorimeter 24 generates monitor color profiles that are compatible with the Kodak/DayStar ColorMatch CMS.

Color management profiles

Many color management software packages (see "Color Management Solutions," later in this chapter) include a module for profiling monitor display characteristics. If your brand of monitor doesn't appear in the CMS's library of preset profiles, some CMSs may be able to generate a custom profile based on information recorded by a compatible hardware calibrator or that you input manually.

Matching Display Color to Input and Output

Adjusting a monitor is only part of the calibration equation. What you see on your screen should be faithful to the way the scanner represents colors. It should also match the colors in any proofing device you may use, as well as the colors of the final output. To make all your equipment components talk to *each other* in the same language, consider a color management software package. But even without a CMS, you can calibrate scanners and printers for internal consistency and coordinate the color characteristics of a single production system manually.

The key to manual system calibration is having some kind of *reference image* that you can pass through the system from input to output. The reference image can be an actual reflective or transparent original (depending on the kind of scanner you're using), or it can be a grayscale or color *target* supplied with your scanner. The latter is preferable, since your sample image may represent less than the full range of colors and/or tones that industry-standard targets contain. Calibrate your system by following these steps:

1. Calibrate your monitor using one of the methods described in this chapter.

2. Calibrate your scanner internally, if necessary. High-end drum, flatbed, and film/transparency scanners calibrate themselves automatically each time you turn them on. Most other scanners require manual calibration approximately once a month to compensate for color shifts that occur over time. Many midrange flatbed scanner manufacturers supply a grayscale or color target with their equipment and include special calibration software.

Tip: Hook up your scanner to a line conditioner to prevent fluctuations in electrical current from influencing CCD readings.

3. Scan the reference image or industry-standard target into the calibrated scanner.

4. Read the 50 percent patch in both grayscale and RGB to ensure that the scanner's gamma is set properly.

5. Compare the image on your monitor with the undigitized original and make further adjustments to the display as necessary.

6. Make sure that your color printer (or color proofing device at an off-site service provider, the film recorder, etc.) is internally calibrated for consistency according to the manufacturer's recommended method.

7. Using your image-editing software, make adjustments for dot gain, CMYK ink balance, paper stock, and other factors that affect color printing output to your chosen device.

8. Output the image to the color proofing device or other medium of your choice.

9. Compare the output results with both the monitor display and the undigitized original and make further adjustments to input and display equipment, if required.

As you can imagine, manual calibration is a trial-and-error process that may require many iterations to produce consistent results. The process becomes even more complicated if you use a variety of input and output devices at multiple locations. Juggling the color diplomacy of so many different standards is a task at which today's color management system (CMS) software excels.

Tip: Scan an 18% gray card or graduated grayscale with a color original and use the scanned image as a calibration target. If the scanned grays have a color cast, you can tweak the target to calibrate your monitor and scanner.

Color Management Systems

The most expensive scanning system in the world won't produce quality color unless all the hardware components in the production chain—scanner, monitor, proofing printer, imagesetter, offset press, or other output device—are talking the same color language. Between the scanner, the monitor, and the output devices, however, color information can easily get mistranslated. You can calibrate all the devices in your system manually, but the process is time-consuming and subjective, and there are no guarantees of color consistency between your system and that of the next party who exchanges files with you.

Color management systems create order out of this chaos by establishing a set of objective rules for communicating color between devices. In order to make the communication "language" universal, a CMS must account for three types of variables, each of which affects color representation at a different level:

- **Gamut**—As explained earlier in this chapter, each *type* of device has a color gamut that is much more limited than the visual spectrum encompassed by CIE color. Scanners, monitors, Photo CD images, digital cameras, film recorders, and television sets represent color in RGB terms, while color printers, proofing devices, and presses use CMYK. A CMS navigates between RGB and CMYK devices using the broader CIE gamut, which contains both RGB and CMYK.

- **Profile**—Two flatbed scanners by different manufacturers rarely reproduce colors in the same way. One scanner may shift hues toward red, while another emphasizes greens. To account for differences in color representation at the brand-name level, a CMS provides preset *profiles* that describe a particular product's color characteristics. Some CMSs also allow you to generate custom profiles for equipment brands for which no profiles exist.

- **Calibration**—If a manufacturer produces 50,000 units of a given scanner model (or monitor, printer, and so on), each one of those units may deviate slightly from the color representation standard specified by the manufacturer. A CMS typically includes calibration options so that you can measure and record any differences between the profile established for your equipment brand and the unique reproduction characteristics of your unit. The CMS can then compensate for these differences when translating color between devices.

> **"**Color management systems create order out of chaos by establishing rules for communicating color between devices.**"**

A color management package's ability to describe *and record* the color characteristics of any input, display, or output device in the workflow (whether or not it is attached to your system) is what makes color consistency possible. Once this information exists digitally, the CMS can retrieve it and use it to negotiate color translations between separate devices in the production chain. Let's take a closer look at the color management process and then survey some of the available color management solutions.

Managing Color—The Process

To use a color management system effectively, you need to follow a defined sequence of steps, which varies depending on the capabilities of a particular package. An ideal CMS procedure would follow this pattern:

1. *Characterize the color performance of the monitor.* Your monitor display mediates between input and output, so record its color characteristics first. Some color management systems provide a full complement of built-in presets from various monitor manufacturers, while others allow you to create a custom monitor profile, either by entering information manually or by using a hardware calibration device.

2. *Calibrate the monitor* so that its white point and other display characteristics match the ideal parameters set forth in the color profile. Many CMS packages customize your monitor's profile at this point to compensate for any variance between your monitor and the standard profile.

Tip: If you output primarily to print media, consider calibrating the monitor white point to the color temperature of the paper stock(s) you print on.

3. *Characterize the scanner or other input device.* If the CMS provides an industry-standard IT8 target like the ones pictured in Figure C–4 in the color gallery, scan it. (If you're using a digital camera, capture an image of the target under controlled lighting conditions.) Open the resulting digital file and let the CMS compare the ideal color and gray tones of the target with the ones your input device generated. The CMS notes any variance and records the information as a digital profile of your scanner's color characteristics for use with future scans.

4. *Use the CMS to transform the target scan to the color space of your monitor.* The CMS now converts the previously scanned image from the scanner's color space to the monitor's color space, using the color profiles it established for both devices. Most color managment systems perform this operation in Adobe Photoshop.

Caution: Every CMS transform causes an image to lose data that can't be recovered. Keep the number of transforms in your workflow to a minimum to avoid unnecessary degradation.

5. *Characterize your color proofer or other output device.* Select or define a profile for the color printer, press conditions, Photo CD, or other output device supported by the CMS.

6. *Output the image file to your chosen output device.* The CMS uses the profiles for monitor and printer (or scanner and printer) to convert image color during this process. Some color management systems allow you to view a "soft proof" (an onscreen CMYK representation) of the image before printing.

Note: Color management packages compensate for a scanner's color characteristics only after an image has already been scanned. They don't transform color on the fly.

Color Management Solutions

The color management steps described in the previous section represent an ideal composite of what a color management system ought to do. Though several CMS products do an especially competent job, no single commercially available CMS conforms perfectly to that ideal. Among current color management systems, common shortcomings include

■ **Inadequate support for the Windows platform**—Most CMS packages (excepting Agfa FotoTune and the Kodak PICC products) are designed for Macintosh only, despite the increased interest in scanning and imaging applications on the Windows platform.

- **Focus on print publishing output**—CMS packages are by and large designed for print publishing professionals. The Kodak-based solutions are notable exceptions in their support for transforming color for Photo CD output.

- **Inconsistent support for display, input, and output profiles**—CMS products vary wildly in the number of preset profiles they provide for monitors, scanners, and printers. Whereas some CMS products ship with huge libraries of device characterizations, others include only a few profiles, forcing you either to do without (risking incorrect color transformations between devices) or to buy additional modules. Some products allow you to create a custom profile if the device you have isn't included among the presets. Keep in mind, too, that there's no single standard for the information that profiles should include.

- **Reliance on specific "industry-standard" applications**—Many CMS products require that you use Photoshop and QuarkXPress in order to obtain the greatest color management benefits. Although this restriction is no restriction for the vast majority of imaging and publishing professionals, it leaves a significant number of potential users out in the cold.

- **Inability to share profile information**—Standards are still under development in the CMS field. Until all CMS manufacturers agree to write their device characterizations in the same way, you may not be able to share profile information with someone else (a client, vendor, or service bureau) who uses a different color management package. Color management initiatives at the operating system level should gradually help to fill in the gaps.

With those limitations in mind, let's take a look at several leading color management packages and their respective strengths.

Caution: Use only one CMS at a time in your system. Leaving multiple CMS products installed results in double correction and introduces new variables into the color conversion process rather than eliminating them.

Color Management at the Operating System Level

Recent initiatives on the Macintosh and Windows platforms to implement color management at the operating system level may go far toward establishing sorely needed standards for describing device color characteristics. Both operating systems support common profile standards put forth by the InterColor Consortium (ICC), an association of major software developers. If these bids toward standardization succeed, scanning and imaging users will be able to share profile information with service bureaus, designers, clients, colleagues in other departments, and other offsite personnel, regardless of which color management system or platform each party is using.

> **"***Recent initiatives to implement color management at the operating system level may go far toward establishing sorely needed standards for describing device color characteristics.***"**

On the Macintosh, version 2 of Apple's ColorSync may help to standardize color management. A partnership between Kodak and Microsoft holds out hope of accomplishing the same goal in Windows 95. What's needed in each case is the support of a sufficient number of device vendors, who must agree to adopt the color description standards that each color management system specifies. The verdict's still out.

Apple ColorSync, Version 2

Released in the spring of 1995 and available through online services, version 2 of Apple's ColorSync is a Macintosh CMS that installs as a systemwide control panel. ColorSync has adopted the ICC standard format for writing device color profile information. Many third-party software and equipment vendors, including Agfa, Canon, Kodak, Light Source, Linotype-Hell, Pantone, PixelCraft, PixelResources, Quark, Radius, and Tektronix, have made commitments to provide ColorSync profile compatibility for new and existing products. The ColorSync ICC format can provide color characterization information across platforms, thus greatly facilitating workflow in multiple-service–provider environments.

Once sufficient third-party support has gathered for the ColorSync 2.0 standard, a typical ColorSync workflow would progress like this:

1. Install the ColorSync-compatible profiles supplied by the manufacturers of your scanner, printer, monitor, and other input and output devices.

2. Scan an image, selecting ColorSync input and output profiles from a pop-up menu. (The host software must support ColorSync in order for the menu to be available.)

3. ColorSync converts the scanner's RGB colors to the CIE color space and then converts this data to the RGB color space of your monitor.

4. Using the LaserWriter 8 PostScript driver, print the image to a PostScript Level 2 color printer that also has a ColorSync profile. Through a designated ColorSync 2 transfer file, PostScript Level 2 printers can color correct image data on the fly during printing without actually altering the data in the file.

ColorSync can also supplement rather than supplant the capabilities of other color management systems. Agfa's FotoTune, for example, can write device profiles both in its own format and in the ICC format supported by ColorSync.

> *❝ColorSync can also supplement rather than supplant the capabilities of other color management systems. ❞*

Color management in Windows 95

Windows publishing and imaging professionals have long lamented the absence of serious color management tools on their platform. Microsoft and Eastman Kodak's Color Management Group hope to provide such tools in the next generation of Microsoft's operating system, so that developers and device manufacturers no longer have to generate their own nonstandardized color management features.

The core of Windows 95's color management architecture, called ICM (for *Image Color Matching* framework), is integrated into monitor and printer setup routines. Windows 95 includes a core group of device profiles, which conform to the same ICC format that Apple's ColorSync also supports. For a full implementation of system-level color management to take place, however, ICM relies on the support of third-party software applications developers and hardware device vendors. Software developers need to modify their applications to call on ICM features, and device vendors need to write their profiles to conform to the ICC format. TIFF, PICT, and EPS file formats may also be redefined so that device profile information can be embedded in image files. When and if all of these developments become reality, color management under Windows 95 will be truly cross-platform. In applications that support ICC profiling, files can then be exchanged between Macintosh and Windows 95 platforms with color fidelity intact.

The default built-in color management application in Windows 95 is the Kodak Color Matching Module (similar to Kodak modules already in use in Adobe Photoshop and PhotoStyler). However, ICM's open architecture allows Windows 95 users to override the Kodak module and substitute another color management application (such as Agfa's FotoTune or Pantone's POCE) of their choice.

Agfa FotoTune

Available on both the Macintosh and Windows platforms, FotoTune version 2 is a well-rounded CMS with a flexible feature set that's suited to service bureau, ad agency, and print shop environments that use Adobe Photoshop and QuarkXPress. FotoTune ships with three targets (one reflective, one transparency, and one 35mm slide) and a veritable host of preset color profiles (which it calls *ColorTags*) for monitors, color printers, film recorders, color spaces, and selected offset press setups. If these aren't enough for your needs, you can use the supplied color characterization utilities to create custom profiles for your devices.

To characterize your monitor, FotoTune requires that you first calibrate it using the Knoll Gamma utility or a hardware calibration device. You then copy Gamma, White Point, and monitor phosphor information from Photoshop's Monitor Setup dialog box and save the settings as a new profile (Figure 5–6).

Preset profile support for scanners is limited to Agfa models only, but you can easily characterize other manufacturers' models. After you scan one of the supplied IT8 targets, FotoTune compares the scanned image values

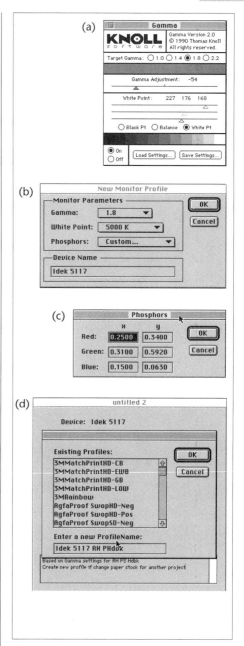

Figure 5–6

Create and save a custom monitor profile (d) in Agfa FotoTune after calibrating your monitor (a) and then entering Gamma, white point (b), and monitor phosphor information (c).

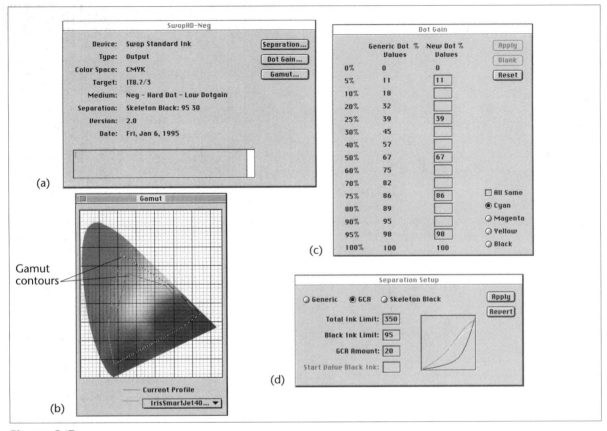

Figure 5–7

FotoTune lets you customize any standard offset printing profile (**a**) with regard to color gamut (**b**), dot gain (**c**), and color separation parameters (**d**). By comparing the color gamut of a proofing device (here, an Iris inkjet printer) to the gamut of specific offset press conditions, you can see how accurately the perceptual output from the proofing printer will match the final output.

with the ones in an Agfa color reference file and records the variance information to disk as a custom profile.

For a color management system to be useful *all* the way through the production process, it should support color conversions and separations, not only to color proofing printers, but also to high-end press proofs and offset press scenarios that take press, paper, and ink considerations into account. In this respect, FotoTune follows through more thoroughly than many CMS products. It supplies

four standard SWOP, as well as four Euro-Ink profiles and multiple ColorTags for digital proofing devices. As shown in Figure 5–7, you can customize any of the offset press profiles, even to the extent of altering settings for color gamut, separation curves, total ink and black ink limits, and dot gain. And you can optionally save any monitor, scanner, or printing profile in the (ICC) format supported by Apple ColorSync 2 and Windows 95.

FotoTune is also flexible in its support for the various directions that a workflow can take. You

Bitmap mode (1 bit), 36K
1 channel, 1 bit per channel

Grayscale mode (8 bits), 284K
1 channel, 8 bits per channel

Indexed color mode (8 bits), 284K
1 channel, 8 bits per channel

RGB mode (24 bits), 852K
3 channels, 8 bits per channel

CMYK mode (32 bits), 1.11MB
4 channels, 8 bits per channel

Figure C–1

© Emil Ihrig

Color depth and file size. *The bit depth (color depth) chosen for scanning affects both the file size and the potential number of color or gray levels in the resulting scanned image. File size increases in proportion to bit depth. The number of colors or gray levels increases exponentially with bit depth. (The black (K) channel in the CMYK color mode is necessary for contouring CMY gamuts in print and does not increase the number of colors in the image.)*

Figure C–2

Dynamic range and detail. A scanner's sensing device determines its sensitivity to light and noise. **Left**: A transparency scanned using a drum scanner (dynamic range: 3.9) shows subtle tonal gradations in the shadow areas of the image—the ribs of the fan, the hand, and the embroidered rose on the apron. **Right**: The same original, when scanned using a CCD-based slide scanner with high-quality sensors and a dynamic range of 3.0, yields excellent results, but the tonal range in shadow areas is slightly compressed.

Figure C–3

Compensating for film emulsion characteristics during Photo CD processing. When the PIW operator processes film using scene balance, color representation is standardized across film types (**left**). When the operator disables scene balance by specifying a universal film term in lock beam mode, the resulting Photo CD scan emphasizes the unique tonal and color characteristics of a specific film emulsion (**right**). Notice the more saturated colors in the right-hand image.

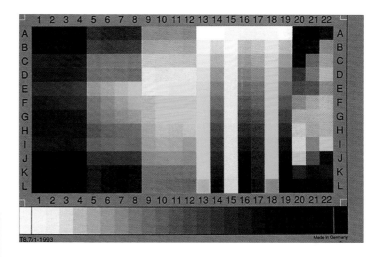

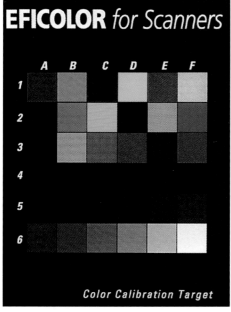

Figure C–4

Color targets for calibration and color management. Color management systems typically supply color reference targets for calibrating and characterizing scanners and other input devices. **Top:** The standard IT8 color target supplied with Agfa FotoTune contains 264 color patches. **Center:** EfiColor Works' scanning target, which contains fewer patches than the industry-standard IT8 targets, is useful for characterizing midrange scanners. **Bottom:** Kodak's IT8 target identifies skin tones among the standard patches.

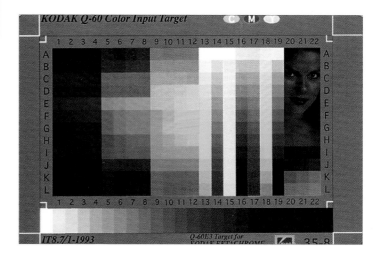

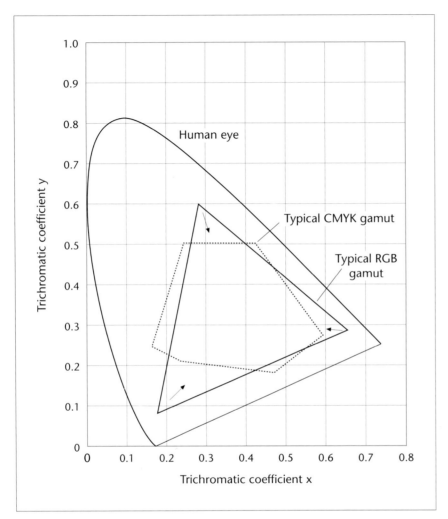
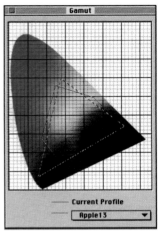

Figure C–5

CIE color space: the basis for color management. Left: *The perceptual CIE color space describes the entire range of colors that the human eye can detect. Since the CIE gamut is much larger than both the RGB and the CMYK gamuts and contains them, it forms the basis for color management systems (CMS) software, which makes it possible to standardize color representation along every step of the production process.* ***Right:*** *This screen from Agfa FotoTune illustrates how the color gamuts of visual perception, input devices, and output devices intersect. The largest shape represents the CIE color gamut; the area within the red lines represents the gamut of a specific set of press conditions; and the area within the dotted lines defines the gamut of an Apple color monitor. Only colors common to all three gamuts can be transferred between devices without loss; translation needs to occur for colors that fall outside the gamuts of one or more devices.*

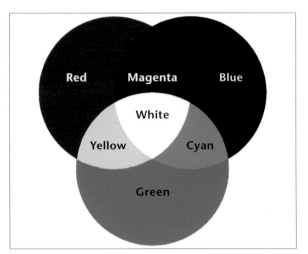

Figure C–6

RGB color model. In the additive RGB color space that describes how digital devices reproduce color, combinations of red, green, and blue produce all available colors by adding light to light. Maximum intensities of red, green, and blue combine to produce white; two-color combinations produce the complementary colors (cyan, magenta, and yellow).

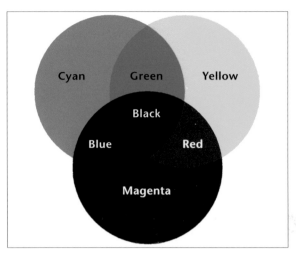

Figure C–7

CMY color model. In the subtractive CMY color space used by the printing industry, cyan, magenta, and yellow combine to generate all printable colors. Theoretically, maximum intensities of CMY should produce pure black. In practice, a muddy brown is produced due to imperfections in ink pigments and a deliberate imbalance toward cyan in the color separation process. Printers therefore use black as a fourth key (K) color to contour the depth of CMY gamuts.

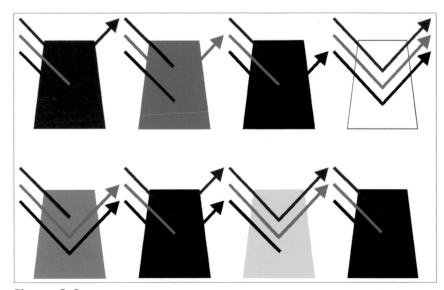

Figure C–8

Subtractive color mixing. When we view colored inks on paper, the red, green, and blue components of white light strike the ink pigments, which trap (absorb) some light waves and reflect others. The reflected light waves make up the colors we see.

Composite color image   © Emil Ihrig

Red channel

Green channel

Blue channel

Figure C–9
RGB color space.
Scanners and computer
monitors "see" colors
as combinations of red,
green, and blue light.
These illustrations of a
young girl wearing a
colorful shirt show how
a composite color
image can be broken
down into its red,
green, and blue
components (channels)
in the RGB color space.

Figure C–10

CMYK color space.
When the composite
color image pictured in
Figure C–9 is rendered
in the CMYK color
space for printing, it
can be broken down
into cyan, magenta,
yellow, and black
components as
shown here. The
distribution of colors
among the four
channels depends on
the press, paper, and
ink parameters for a
particular print job.

Cyan channel

Magenta channel

Yellow channel

Black channel

© Emil Ihrig

Figure C–11

Tonal character. The tonal character of an original determines which details should be emphasized for scanning. **Top**: High-key images contain the details of interest predominantly in the diffuse highlight tones. To emphasize these light details, scan high-key originals using a Gamma value between 1.2 and 1.3. **Center**: Balanced originals emphasize detail either throughout the tonal range or in the midtones. Scan them using a Gamma value between 1.4 and 1.6. **Bottom**: Low-key originals emphasize subjects in shadow areas. To bring out available detail in those darker tones, scan them using a Gamma value between 1.6 and 1.9.

© Emil Ihrig

© Emil Ihrig

20 lpi

75 lpi

Figure C–12

Halftone screen frequency and detail. Detail in a printed image is a function of the halftone screen frequency—the number of halftone dots per linear inch. Provided the printer resolution is high enough to support a full 256 tones per channel at the line screen requested, increasing the screen frequency enhances the appearance of continuous tone.

150 lpi

© Emil Ihrig

225 ppi, 150 lpi (1.5:1 ppi-to-lpi ratio)

© Emil Ihrig

Figure C–13

Resolution-to-screen-frequency ratio and image quality. Including excess pixels in an image doesn't improve print quality. This is because the RIP (raster image processor) of a PostScript output device produces only one tone (one dot) per halftone cell, regardless of how many pixels make up each cell. The RIP averages the tones of all the pixels in each cell to arrive at the single-tone value. When an image contains more pixels per cell than necessary, this averaging process takes more processing time, costs more money, and can sometimes result in softened contrast. A halftoning factor of 1.5:1 (*top*) is adequate to reproduce tones accurately, as can be seen in comparisons with images at higher resolutions (*center, bottom*).

450 ppi, 150 lpi (3:1 ppi-to-lpi ratio)

800 ppi, 150 lpi (5.33 ppi-to-lpi ratio)

Figure C–14

Interpolation for resampling.
*The sophistication of an interpolation algorithm makes a difference in the visible quality of an image that has been resampled. The uppermost image was scanned at a resolution appropriate for printing at the desired output dimensions. The bottom three images were scanned at half the required resolution and then resampled up to the necessary output resolution using three different interpolation algorithms. Photoshop's **Nearest Neighbor** interpolation method is the fastest but produces jagged edges between adjacent tones. **Bicubic** interpolation is the slowest method but delivers the sharpest results of the three. **Bilinear** interpolation produces the softest results, avoiding the artifacts that the Bicubic method sometimes introduces.*

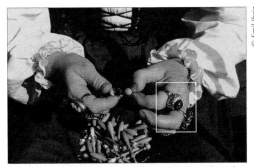

Scanned at correct resolution, uninterpolated

Detail

Nearest neighbor interpolation

Detail

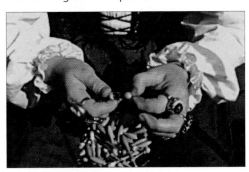

Bilinear interpolation

Detail

Bicubic interpolation

Detail

© Emil Ihrig

Full-range image (0% to 100%)

Highlight: 4%; Shadow: 95%

Highlight: 7%; Shadow: 90%

Highlight: 10%; Shadow: 78%

Figure C–15

Adjusting highlight and shadow points. *When an image is destined for print output, the tonal range must be compressed in order to compensate for specific press, paper stock, and ink parameters. Adjusting the highlight and shadow points achieves this compression so that details don't muddy in the darkest areas or drop out to white in the lightest tones. But as these examples show, adjusting highlight and shadow values flattens overall image contrast as tonal compression increases. Gamma and curve adjustment (see Figure C–16) overcomes this limitation by re-introducing eye-pleasing contrast in the tonal ranges that need it most.*

© Emil Ihrig

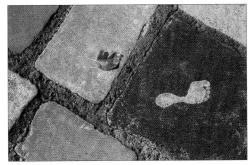
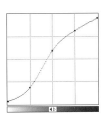
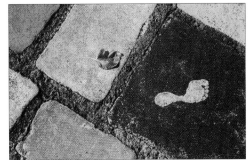

© Emil Ihrig

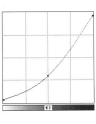

© Emil Ihrig

Figure C–16

Enhancing detail using tone curves. To enhance contrast and detail during input, shape a tone curve for scanning based on the tonal character of the original. **Top**: High-key originals require darkening in the three-quarter tones and midtones, but not in the quarter tones. **Center**: For balanced images that are well exposed, create an S-shaped curve in which three-quarter tones are darkened and quarter tones are brightened. Midtones may need to be brightened or darkened depending on the content of the original. **Bottom**: Brighten the three-quarter tones, midtones, and quarter tones of low-key originals.

(a)

(b)

© Emil Ihrig

Figure C–17

Strategies for eliminating color casts before input. Most scanner interfaces offer a variety of tools for removing color casts from an image, including tone curves, hue and saturation controls, color balance controls, color wheels, and white and black point eyedroppers. The examples shown here feature the tools offered by the Polaroid SprintScan 35. (*a*) This original has a blue cast that pervades all tonal ranges of the image and is especially obvious in the highlights and midtones.
(*b*) After setting the white point using the SprintScan 35's Eyedropper tool and Highlight Point dialog box, excess blue is removed from the image. Highlights appear whiter and midtones (instrument, bow) appear warmer. (*c*) Color saturation sliders offer another intuitive technique for eliminating unwanted color casts. (*d*) Channel-by-channel contrast, brightness, and gamma adjustments, such as the SprintScan 35's Contrast/ Brightness dialog box pictured here, can also help eliminate color casts. (*e*) The Highlight Point dialog box is designed for removing color casts from highlight tones.

(c)

(d)

(e)

Figure C–18

*Enhancing color for the sake of content. The subject matter of an original and its eventual use often determine how colors should be altered. Using a scanner's hue and saturation controls, you can sometimes improve on the colors of the original. **Top**: The greenery and fall leaves in this original appear dull. **Bottom**: Globally darkening reds and yellows and increasing the saturation of red through the prescan controls produces these more intense, dramatic colors.*

© Emil Ihrig

Figure C–19

Sharpening the prescan. The scanning process softens images slightly, so some sharpening is necessary either as a pre-processing or a post-processing step. Not all scanners give the user as much precise control over sharpening as leading image-editing packages do. Unsharp Masking options in a scanner interface are especially tricky because oversharpening can lead to unsightly "halos." **Top:** An unsharpened scanned image. **Center:** Optimal sharpening produces an eye-pleasing balance between contrast and detail. **Bottom:** Oversharpening pushes contrast to the extreme, leading to loss of detail and an artificial look.

© Emil Ihrig

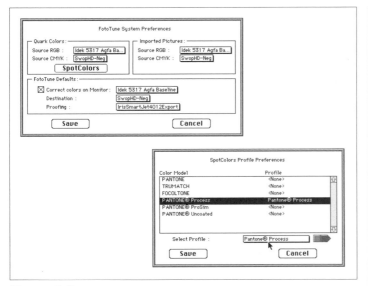

Figure 5–8

*The FotoTune System Preferences dialog box in QuarkXPress lets you correct for solid colors and imported image colors and specify correction profiles for monitor display, proofing, and offset press output (**top**). It also supports profiles for popular spot color models (**bottom**).*

can correct a scan for monitor display, edit the image in Photoshop, and then generate CMYK separations using an output profile (which FotoTune optionally can save as a custom Photoshop separation table). If you plan to place a scanned image directly into a layout, you can choose instead to convert from an RGB scanner color space directly to the final offset press color space. You can also generate an onscreen CMYK soft proof in Photoshop or QuarkXPress. In QuarkXPress, FotoTune lets you correct solid and spot colors as well as image colors, covering every step from monitor correction to proofing to final output (Figure 5–8). And to boost productivity, FotoTune lets you create direct device-to-device conversions called *ColorLinks*, which bypass the intermediate conversion to CIE color space, thereby reducing the number of transformations and accelerating the color conversion process.

DayStar/Kodak ColorMatch

Eastman Kodak and DayStar Digital, joint developers of ColorMatch, started from the premise that most Macintosh imaging professionals use Photoshop, QuarkXPress, or a combination of the two for input, editing, and output. ColorMatch works directly from within these applications to control color transformations for a variety of well-thought-out workflow scenarios.

ColorMatch is useful for professionals who work in several input and output media because it includes profiles (called *precision transforms* in the Kodak lingo) for Photo CD, film recorders, and a device-independent RGB color space, as well as for monitors, flatbed and slide scanners, and color proofing devices. Another ColorMatch strength is the ability to preseparate color TIFF files from within Photoshop, which means that you can output those color separations from page composition programs other than QuarkXPress.

On the other hand, ColorMatch is a little weak on scanner characterization. It provides only a few default scanner profiles and offers no utilities for calibrating scanners or creating custom profiles. You can overcome this flaw by supplementing ColorMatch with Kodak's compatible Precision Input Color Characterization software (described later in this chapter). ColorMatch does supply an extensive bundle of monitor profiles, but if your monitor is not included among them, you can perform only limited visual calibration using the included ColorSet utility (Figure 5–9). Again, there are workarounds. You can use the DayStar Colorimeter 24 or any Kodak-compatible calibration utility to generate custom monitor profiles.

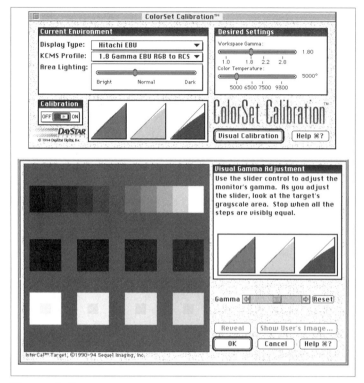

Figure 5–9

*The ColorSet utility supplied with DayStar's ColorMatch lets you select a monitor profile, adjust for ambient lighting (**top**), and perform visual Gamma adjustment by tweaking brightness and contrast controls while viewing a patented digital target (**bottom**).*

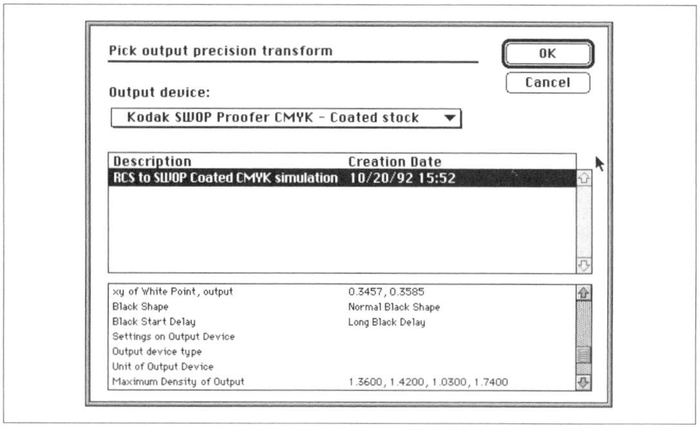

In Photoshop, color management workflow can take several forms. You can color correct Photo CD images or previously scanned images to match either the display or final output; transfer images faithfully between systems with different monitors by using a device-independent Interchange RGB format; create an onscreen "soft proof" preview prior to generating color separations; and color separate images into CMYK TIFF format for direct printing or export to QuarkXPress or other layout packages. Figures 5–10 and 5–11 show some of the steps involved in these processes.

Tip: *If you plan to place an image directly into a layout and don't need to edit it onscreen, you achieve the highest quality results by transforming color from the scanner or Photo CD color space directly to the color space of the final output device, bypassing display correction entirely.*

When using ColorMatch withQuarkXPress, you can import and color correct Photo CD and

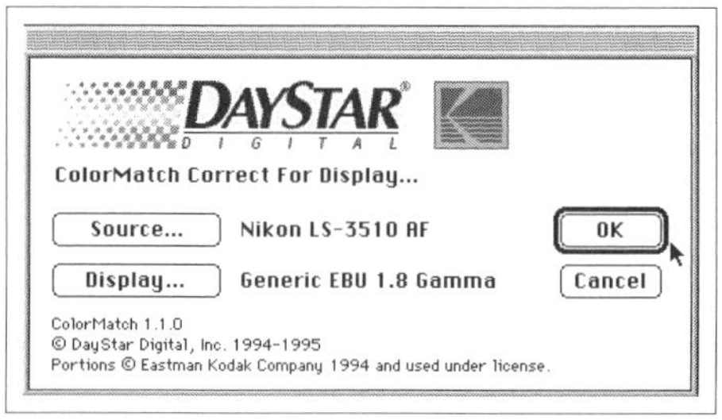

Figure 5–10

ColorMatch lets you simulate CMYK output onscreen from within Photoshop, based on the color profile for your chosen output device.

Figure 5–11

The ColorMatch Correct for Display command in Photoshop uses source and destination profiles to color correct a scanned image so that the display closely matches the undigitized original.

scanned images on the fly; simulate a CMYK preview for both imported images and solid colors; and allow ColorMatch to color correct the entire document during printing. Alternatively, you can simply import images that have been preseparated by ColorMatch in Photoshop and print them without invoking any ColorMatch commands.

EfiColor Works

This low-cost CMS for the Macintosh provides an especially large quantity of preset profiles for proofing devices, press conditions, and monitors. It supports only a small number of scanners directly, but generating and customizing a profile for any device is an easy process with the intuitive Profile Editor. EfiColor Works' profiles are ColorSync compliant, which is good news for scanning professionals who often transfer images between systems and need standardized color reference information.

To create a custom monitor characterization, you open one of EfiColor Works' standard monitor profiles, edit white point, gamma, and phosphor information, and save the profile under an appropriate new name. Basic scanner characterization is also straightforward. You scan the target illustrated in Figure C–4 in the color gallery, save it as a TIFF file, open the TIFF in EfiColor for Scanners, place the test squares over the scanned patches as shown in Figure 5–12, and save the file under a name that reflects the scanner name and date. When you open a scanned image in Photoshop and select the EfiColor Filter, you can then match the display colors to the original unscanned image by selecting the ColorSync-compliant scanner profile in the "From" category and the monitor profile in the "To" category (Figure 5–13).

For creating color separations in Photoshop, EfiColor Works provides a large library of Photoshop-compatible color separation tables based on various Gray Component Replacement (GCR) and rendering style (photographic or solid-color) settings. All of these are also customizable. To color separate an RGB file you need only make sure that the appropriate separation table is loaded (Figure 5–14) and then select CMYK from Photoshop's Mode menu.

EfiColor Works supports QuarkXPress through both the EfiColor XTension and the EfiColor EPS XTension. Using the EfiColor Preferences dialog box, you can specify systemwide or documentwide input and output profiles to use when importing preseparated images from Photoshop or generating color separations from Quark. The EfiColor EPS XTension also lets you manage color for EPS and DCS (*desktop color separation*) files imported from vector illustration packages. Within a document, you can edit these settings on a picture-by-picture basis.

Figure 5–12

Characterizing a scanner with EfiColor for Scanners: fitting the selection marquees within the patches of the scanned target tells the program the locations of critical color areas.

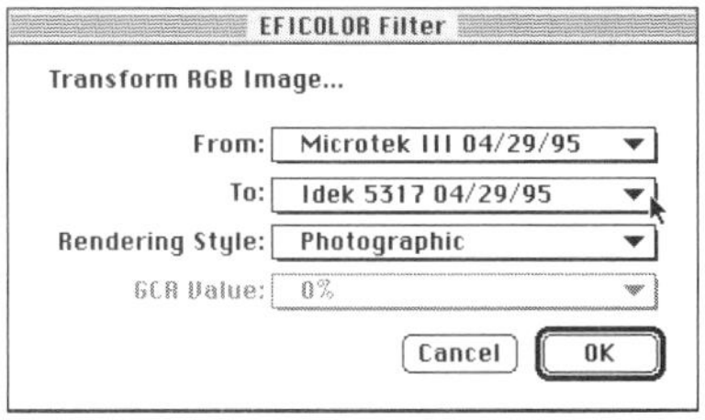

Figure 5–13

In Photoshop, the EfiColor filter can compensate for variations between the unscanned original, the scanner color space, and the monitor color space.

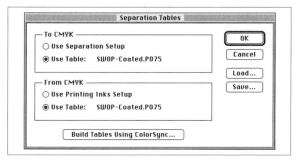

Figure 5–14

Each of the separation tables that EfiColor Works supplies for use with Photoshop is based on a particular printing device or set of offset press conditions, photographic rendering style, and preferred amount of GCR.

Among the most useful features of EfiColor Works is the ability to fine-tune color management for press conditions using the Profile Editor. As Figure 5–15 shows, you can customize any printer or press conditions profile extensively.

Kodak CMS Solutions

Kodak, one of the few color management vendors to support the Windows and Macintosh platforms equally, believes in a modular approach to color management. It offers several partial solutions that you can combine to build a complete CMS. If you use Adobe Photoshop, you can access any of the modules you have purchased by using the Kodak CMS Acquire command in Photoshop's File menu.

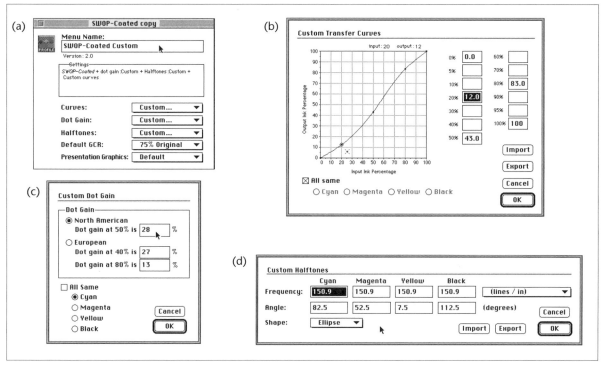

Figure 5–15

Using EfiColor Works' Profile Editor, you can customize printer or offset press conditions profiles (a) with regard to transfer functions (b), dot gain (c), and halftone settings (d).

Device Color Profile Starter Pack (DCP)/ Precision Color Management System

The Device Color Profile (DCP) Starter Pack is geared exclusively toward providing display and output color correction for Photo CD images. As the Kodak Precision Color Management System (KPCMS), it is built into Adobe Photoshop, where users can access it through the File:Open command. Users of other imaging applications that accept Photoshop-compatible plug-ins can obtain the Pack directly from Kodak.

When you open a Photo CD image, the DCP or Kodak CMS asks you to select two device profiles (precision transforms)—one for input and the other for output. The input profile, or *source precision transform*, is a Photo CD device based on the type of processing that the Photo CD service provider used. The output profile, or *destination precision transform*, can be a monitor, a color proofer, or a copier as shown in Figure 3–20 in Chapter 3. If you plan to edit the image onscreen before printing it, choose a monitor profile to color correct the Photo CD image for your display. On the other hand, if the image doesn't need editing and you plan to print it or place it directly into a layout, choose a color proofer profile as the destination transform.

Precision Input Color Characterization (PICC)

Kodak's Precision Input Color Characterization (PICC) module, available for both Macintosh and Windows, augments the capabilities of the basic Device Color Profile Starter Pack by providing a scanner calibration utility. PICC includes both a reflective and a transparent version of a standard IT8 color target. After you scan the target, PICC evaluates the accuracy of the scan and generates a characterization profile (a *precision transform*) for your scanner. This profile is in the same format as other precision transforms used by the Kodak Acquire module supplied with Adobe Photoshop. Place it in the KPCMS folder or directory to make it automati-cally available for use whenever you call up Kodak Acquire.

To use your custom precision transform in Photoshop, choose Kodak Acquire from the File menu. Select the scanner transform as the source and a monitor or printer profile as the destination. Acquire next takes you to the software supplied with your scanner, where you scan as usual. Kodak Acquire then transforms the color in the scanned image as a post-processing step, using your source and destination selections. If you choose to color correct for monitor display, you can use Acquire again later to transform the image from monitor to proofer color space when you're ready to print. To avoid unnecessary image degradation, however, apply as few color transformations during the workflow as possible.

Tip: *To calibrate and create a custom profile for Photo CD color, send Kodak's IT8 target with your photos for Photo CD processing.*

PCS100 kit

For high-end Macintosh imaging and scanning applications, Kodak offers the PCS100 kit, which includes Kodak device profiles, a PICC-like scanner characterization utility, a 16-bit monitor calibration device, and a NuBus acceleration card to speed the color transform process for Photo CD and Pro Photo CD images. With PCS100, you also can create direct custom links between devices, which skips the intermediate conversion to CIE color space and saves time for each conversion. These custom links are useful when you repeatedly use the same scanner/monitor, scanner/printer, or monitor/printer combination.

Monaco Color

Monaco Color (Figure 5–16) is a modular color management system for the Macintosh that can be adapted to low- or high-end needs according to your budget. Supplied as two Photoshop plug-ins, it includes a strong scan-

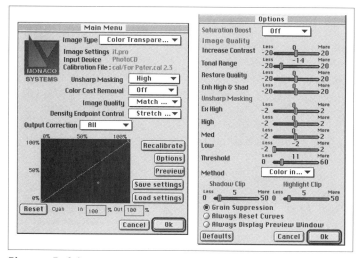

Figure 5–16

Monaco Color features intelligent image enhancement functions as part of the color management process.

Figure 5–17   *courtesy Light Source Corp.*

Light Source's Colortron combines the functions of a colorimeter, densitometer, and spectrophotometer to match specific colors from input to output.

ner characterization utility but provides no direct support for monitor characterization and calibration, so there's no guarantee that what you see on your screen matches either the scanner or the printed image. However, Monaco Color excels at correcting for final output. It handles automatic image-enhancement functions, color-cast compensation, unsharp masking, and batch processing as part of the color management process.

Light Source Colortron

Unlike CMS software, the pocket-size Colortron from Light Source Computer Images, Inc. (Figure 5–17) doesn't try to take on the task of managing all the colors in the visible spectrum at one time. Instead, it aims at something closer to the practical hearts of commercial print publishing professionals—matching specific colors on a project-by-project basis. The Colortron scientifically measures the exact spectral data of any object and saves the data to disk in a format that's compatible with ColorSync and many other CMS products. This means that the spectral data, say, for a restaurant tablecloth can be saved as a profile and transferred to a computer monitor, where it might be exactly matched to a paper stock for the restaurant's menu. Since the Colortron can measure reflective, transmissive, and

ambient light, it can compensate for how an item is viewed at different times of the day or under different lighting conditions.

Beyond Color Management

Good color management can go a long way toward solving output problems, but by itself it can't make an image perfect. Depending on the conditions of the original image and the goals set for your final project, your scans may require additional work before they're ready for output. Color enhancement, sharpening, and compensation for potential halftoning problems are just a few of the steps that you often need to perform *after* scanning takes place. Chapter 6 describes how best to evaluate source images before scanning them so that you can obtain the best scan possible. Chapter 8 addresses other aspects of image enhancement.

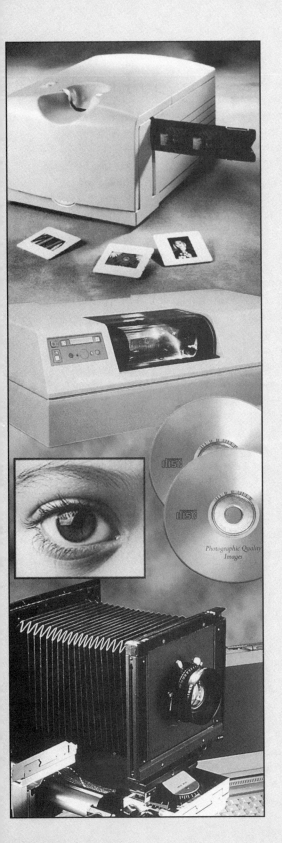

Evaluating Source Images

Three factors determine the quality of a scan—the technology behind the digitizing equipment, the skill of the scanning operator, and the characteristics of the source image. All too often, we discount the importance of source images, assuming that the scanner and the retouching expert can work miracles all by themselves. Yet, even with the most expensive scanner and the most experienced operator at your disposal, no amount of scanner acrobatics or digital darkroom magic can compensate fully for a poor-quality original.

Knowing how to evaluate an original before you scan it helps ensure that the source image translates into the highest quality scan possible. Information about the physical condition, tonal character, exposure, focus, and medium of an original can indicate whether or not it's usable. Proper evaluation can also guide you in choosing scanning settings that optimize the best features of an image while playing down any inherent problems. Finally, this information can suggest steps you may need to take later in order to further correct and enhance the images after scanning. Read on for guidance about how to make the most of the tools and techniques for inspecting source images for your scans.

The Right Tools for the Job

In this digital age, you're supposed to do everything by computer, right? Not quite. There are a few "analog" tools that still can come in handy when your goal is to evaluate (and, sometimes, to repair) original artwork that's destined for scanning. Graphic arts professionals with a strong background in photography probably are already familiar with most of these. Here's a brief rundown of each tool and its uses (see Figure 6–1 for examples of some of these):

- *Light table*—Light tables, ranging in size from 8 × 10 inches to 48 × 72 inches or larger, are invaluable for examining transmissive art such as 35mm slides or larger transparencies. They illuminate the artwork from beneath, making colors and imperfections easier to see. Most light tables use a fluorescent light source with a *daylight-corrected* color temperature of 5,000 degrees Kelvin (see Chapter 5 for more information about the importance of color temperature in maintaining ideal viewing conditions).

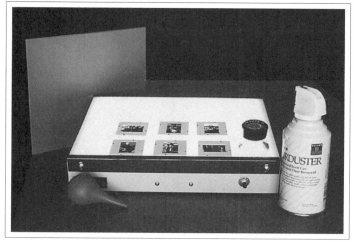

Figure 6–1   © Emil Ihrig

Light tables, 18% gray cards, air blowers, loupes, and canned air are essential basic tools for inspecting and evaluating original artwork.

- *Viewing booth*—A viewing booth or other light source that maintains a consistent 5,000-degree Kelvin color temperature is standard for viewing reflective artwork such as photographic prints and hand-drawn illustrations. Color prepress houses often have these to evaluate press sheets for customer approval prior to the final press run.

- *Loupe*—A loupe is a small magnifier that fits between the thumb and forefinger and is useful for examining tiny details and imperfections in original artwork. Photographers, professional lithographers, and color separators use loupes to evaluate scanner and camera films, printing plates, and press sheets. Loupe magnification factors range from 4X to 22X; an 8X or 10X loupe is adequate for most evaluation needs.

- *Air blower, blower brush, canned air*—Removing debris from sensitive film or transparency emulsions is a delicate operation best handled by blowing air on the original (see the "Dust and Debris" section of this chapter). A common bulb-shaped air blower is suitable for this purpose, as is the chemical propellant known as "canned air." For removal of dust from slightly less-sensitive materials like reflective prints, you can sometimes use a blower brush.

Caution: *When using canned air, hold the container totally upright to keep the propellant from discharging onto and ruining the original artwork.*

- *18% gray card*—Available at photographic supply stores, an 18% gray card is useful when you're inspecting a photo for subtle color casts. Its 50 percent gray surface tonality provides a precise neutral standard against which you can gauge the purity of whites and grays in the original. (The 18% refers to the percentage of ambient light *reflected* by the card.)

Evaluating Physical Condition

More often than not, originals reach you in less than perfect physical condition. Slides and transparencies arrive unprotected, covered with dust, lint, scratches, and enough fingerprints to frame any crime suspect. Reflective prints or illustrations are shipped with crimps, folds, and smudges. Careless handling is at the root of most of these problems, but that doesn't relieve the scanner operator of the responsibility to eliminate them. Scanners are notorious for amplifying existing physical flaws in an original, so the more of these you can remove before scanning, the less agony you'll suffer doing time consuming retouching later.

Tip: Always handle originals by their edges to prevent introduction of scratches, fingerprints, crimping, or other flaws. And never attach paper clips to photographic prints or transparencies.

Dust and Debris

Dust, lint, hair, and similar debris attach themselves to originals all too easily. If you don't remove them before scanning, they produce speckled effects and artifacts like the ones shown in Figure 6–2. Such artifacts show up

Dust artifacts, close-up

Dust on original

Dust removed

© Emil Ihrig

Figure 6–2
Dust on original artwork produces unsightly speckling if it isn't removed before scanning.

prominently on transmissive media (slides, transparencies, and negative film) because light passes directly through them during scanning, and any dust or scratches are amplified.

Fortunately, dust and debris are the easiest types of physical flaws to deal with. You can remove most dust with the help of either an air blower or a can of compressed air held upright. You can also use a blower brush, but only if the bristles are extremely soft—touching film originals with coarser bristles can introduce scratches to the gelatin emulsion. And if you're storing originals for scanning at a later date, take measures to shield them against collecting further dust. Use protective antistatic sleeves for slides and transparencies, and sandwich reflective originals between cardboard backings.

Caution: *Keep the drum or flatbed platen of your scanner immaculate at all times. If dust and debris are present in the scanner mechanism, they tend to make the magnetic leap to any originals that come in contact with it. The scanner lens also has to "look through" the dust at the originals.*

Removing Dust and Debris After the Fact

If all your protective efforts fail and dust or lint makes its way onto the scanned image, there are several image-editing techniques you can use to retouch it later. (These techniques work well for scratches, too.) Some production artists like the simplicity of Photoshop's Dust & Scratches filter, but settings need careful adjustment to prevent excessive blurring of an image in the interest of smoothing out differences in neighboring tones. For best results, apply this filter to small selected areas at a time and follow it up with an unsharp masking or edge-sharpening filter. Cloning tools can help you remove artifacts locally by reproducing unblemished parts of the image in the affected areas. If dust or debris pervades the

image, try using a low setting of Photoshop's Median filter—which offers intuitive control over the degree of blurring that takes place—followed by an application of Unsharp Mask or Sharpen Edges. Figure 6–3 shows examples of each of these approaches.

Scratches and Crimps

Careless packaging and handling of originals can lead to the introduction of scratches, folds, and crimps. As with dust and debris, these are more likely to show up in the scanned image if the original was a slide, transparency, or negative film, due to static electricity.

You often can alleviate folds and crimps before scanning by sandwiching the original between protective covers, placing an evenly dispersed weight on top, and leaving the artwork to flatten for awhile. This certainly requires less patience than trying to reconstruct image information lost when covered over by half-moon–shaped crimp artifacts.

Eliminating scratches from originals is more difficult. If the scratches pass through areas where important details are located, try to obtain undamaged copy of the artwork or face the prospect of reconstructing the damaged details digitally with uncertain results. In the case of transmissive media, if the scratches appear in less important areas of the image *and* are located on the *substrate* (the back side of the film) rather than on the emulsion side, you may be able to make them less visible by gingerly applying a tiny bit of petroleum jelly. See the foregoing section, "Removing Dust and Debris After the Fact," for hints on how to handle scratches and crimps after you've already scanned an image.

Fingerprints

Fingerprints are more challenging to remove than other artifacts because they consist of skin oils that can change the qualities (and colors)

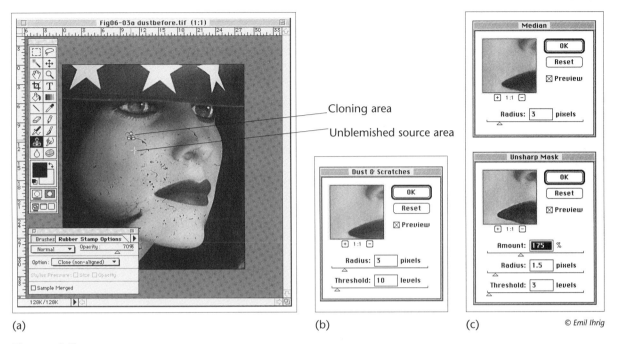

Cloning area

Unblemished source area

© Emil Ihrig

Figure 6–3

Approaches to removing dust, lint, and scratches. (a) Cloning tools can cover up unsightly speckles by copying areas with similar tonal values to the areas marred by artifacts. (b) Photoshop's Dust & Scratches filter smoothes out artifacts by altering tonal values according to user-selectable settings based on relative contrast (threshold) and distance (radius). (c) Photoshop's Median filter averages the brightness values of pixels within a user-specified radius. When followed by an application of the Unsharp Mask or Sharpen Edges filter, it can remove dust and scratches without noticeably compromising image sharpness.

of sensitive film emulsion on contact. Assuming the fingerprints are located on the substrate of the film, you may be able to remove them by carefully daubing the film with a lint- and scratch-free applicator moistened in a film cleaner or denatured alcohol solution. However, if the fingerprints appear on the emulsion side of the film, chances are that the oils (and patterns) have already been permanently absorbed into the content of the image. Be prepared to spend hours retouching and color correcting the scan if you can't obtain another undamaged copy of the original. Follow the example of photofinishing professionals and always handle film wearing lintless, white cotton gloves (available from photo supply stores).

Evaluating Tonal Character and Exposure

Once you've finished examining an original for physical defects, your next task is to determine the way in which detail is distributed among available brightness levels in the image. There are actually two processes involved here. First, you must determine which portions of the tonal range contain the most important details in the image. These define the *tonal character* or *key* of the original. Then, you need to evaluate whether the image is properly *exposed*—whether the brightness levels throughout the image are appropriate for emphasizing the details in those important subject areas. Both tonal character and exposure have a significant impact on the settings you choose during scanning, as well as image-editing decisions that you make later to optimize image output.

High-Key, Low-Key, and Balanced Images

You can classify the tonal character of any original as high key, low key, or balanced. The subject matter, the intention of the artist or photographer, and (for photographic originals) the time of day when the image was captured all help determine which tonal character applies to a particular image. Figure C–11 in the color gallery depicts examples of high-key, low-key, and balanced images.

- In *high-key* or *snow* images, the subjects to be emphasized appear in the highlight tones. A photograph of a polar bear in the snow at midday, for example, contains the most important details in bright, near-white areas such as the bear's fur. These lighter tones are sometimes called *diffuse highlights*. Midtone and shadow areas of high-key images contain relatively little detail of interest.

- *Low-key* or *night* images feature the most important details in shadow areas, with less emphasis on subjects in the midtones and highlights. Photos of city scenes after dark are good examples of low-key images.

- *Balanced* (midtone) images, in which details of interest are either distributed evenly from dark to light or are concentrated in colors and tones of medium brightness, are by far the most common type you'll encounter.

If you're experienced at examining originals for scanning, you can probably determine tonal character by visual inspection alone. Grayscale originals are easy to evaluate in this respect because the tones of a single color—black—are involved. Analyzing tonal distribution in color originals is a less intuitive process, since hues and saturation levels can confuse the eye's perception of brightness. Fortunately, most software packages that accompany midrange and higher-end scanners supply a histogram utility that analyzes the tonal character of the original before you scan it. We used UMAX MagicScan, which accompanies the UMAX PowerLook, for the examples in this chapter.

Analyzing a Prescan Histogram

A *histogram* is simply a visual map of the way in which tones are distributed throughout an image. Many scanning plug-ins allow you to prescan an undigitized original and then generate a histogram. You can use the information in the histogram as a basis for decisions about how to alter the image's tone curve during scanning to emphasize the most important details.

The horizontal axis of a histogram shows the distribution of tones running from dark (left) to light (right), while the vertical axis shows how large a proportion of the image is assigned to each tone. As Figure 6–4 indicates, histograms of low-key images show a heavier vertical emphasis toward the left side of the tonal map; histograms of balanced images tend to follow a bell curve with the high point near the center; and histograms of high-key images display the highest proportion of tonal values toward the right side of the map. Blank areas at either end of the histogram indicate a complete absence of detail in the established highlights or shadows; tones in the image need to be remapped to those areas.

Altering Tonal Curve or Gamma Value Based on Image Key

What does the tonal distribution of an original have to do with decisions about how to scan it? Plenty. For various reasons, most forms of

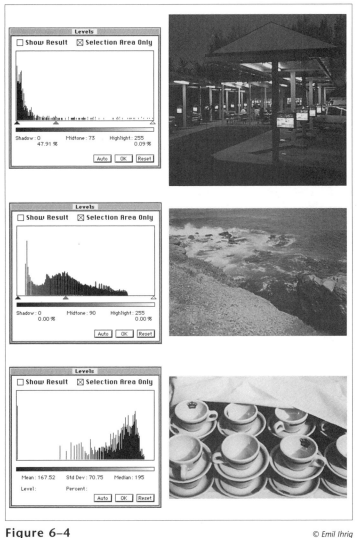

Figure 6–4

© Emil Ihrig

*Prescan histograms (in these examples, from UMAX MagicScan) show the tonal character of an undigitized original. **Top to bottom:** The prescan histograms for a low-key original, a balanced (midtone) original, and a high-key original.*

output can't reproduce all the tones in an original—commercial print media are limited by CMYK ink gamuts and paper stock characteristics, multimedia images have a restricted color range, and video images must compromise between color depth and frame resolution. Given these limitations, you have to pick and choose what's

important in an original and scan in a way that will emphasize those details at the expense of compressing others. Understanding the tonal character of an original can guide you to choosing scanner settings that don't compromise output quality.

Many software packages that accompany midrange and higher-end scanners allow you to manipulate either the *tonal curve* or *gamma value* of the original (or both) during scanning. Both of these techniques accomplish the same task, that of redistributing the existing tonal values in the original; it's just that a tonal curve gives you a graphical representation of the process, whereas editing the gamma value forces you to be content with a numerical one. As Figure 6–5 demonstrates, a perfectly diagonal tonal curve represents a baseline, unaltered distribution of tonal values. Altering this curve redistributes those values, enhancing the level of detail in some tonal ranges while compressing that level in others. (You can't have it both ways—a gain in the highlights requires a loss in the shadows, and vice versa.) Assuming a curve in which horizontal values progress from light at the left to dark at the right, here's how to edit the prescan tonal curve based on the key of the original image:

- *Low-key originals*—Drag the curve downward from the center and/or lower left to enhance detail in the shadows and midtones, compressing or eliminating detail in the highlights.

- *High-key originals*—Drag the curve upward from the center and/or

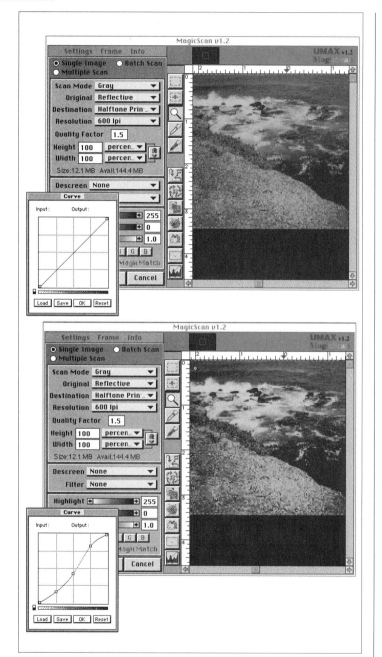

Figure 6–5

© Emil Ihrig

*To bring out detail as dictated by the tonal character of the original, edit its tonal curve prior to scanning. **Top:** an unaltered prescan and histogram in UMAX MagicScan. **Bottom:** the same prescan after an S-curve has been applied to enhance detail in the midtones and shadows.*

upper right to enhance detail in the highlights and midtones, compressing or eliminating the amount of detail in the shadows.

■ *Balanced originals*—If they're well exposed, alter the curve very little. If more contrast is necessary, you can create a nearly S-shaped curve like the one in Figure 6–5, which compresses detail in the highlights and shadows and lightens the midtones slightly to compensate for dot gain on a printing press.

Note: *Reverse these instructions when the scanner interface depicts tonal range as progressing from dark at the left, to light at the right.*

Tonal curves offer you more control than numerical gamma values, since you can edit tonal distribution at many points along the tonal range. But if your scanning software interface allows you only to enter a single numerical gamma value, set the gamma to 1.8 or higher for low-key images, 1.2 or lower for high-key images, and near 1.5 for balanced midtone images.

Evaluating Exposure

Exposure describes the degree to which a photographic original successfully captures all of the important detail that the creator of the image intended. You might say that the relationship between tonal character and exposure is like the relationship between intent and execution—sometimes your intentions are carried out to the letter, and sometimes the execution falls short of expectations.

When an image is darker overall than it should be and lacks detail in the shadow tones, it's underexposed. If the original is brighter overall than it should be and details in the highlights are washed out, it's overexposed. Imagine photographing that polar bear in the snow under very bright sunlight: the resulting overexposed image would show only pure white (lack of detail) where individual bristles of fur should appear.

Judicious setting of gamma values and/or tonal curves during scanning can compensate partially for a poorly exposed original (Figure 6–6). We say "partially" because the results depend on whether the shadows or highlights were completely washed out to black or white, respectively. Let the prescan histogram be your guide. If the histogram shows no tones at all at one end of the spectrum, you can certainly redistribute available tones to introduce some color or gray shades into the affected areas, but you can't manufacture "true" detail that wasn't there in the first place. The prognosis is better for originals that may be dark or light but where some highlight or shadow detail exists; in these cases, it's simply a matter of brightening or darkening the affected tonal ranges to bring out the latent detail.

Checking for Color Casts

A *color cast* is an undesirable bias toward a certain hue that pervades an entire image. Photographic originals are often subject to them. The

Figure 6–6 © Emil Ihrig

*Editing the tonal curve of poorly exposed originals can improve the level of detail in important subject areas, provided that a full range of tones is available. Here, the curve of a balanced but underexposed original (**top**) is edited (**center**) to bring out detail in midtones and shadows (**bottom**).*

lighting conditions under which an image was captured, the unique color characteristics of a given brand of film, and anomalies during processing can all contribute to shifts toward yellow, blue, green, or red. If the color cast is extreme, you will almost certainly notice it, but subtle color casts are less easy to perceive. The best method for detecting them is to hold up a printed grayscale or an 18% gray card (available through photographic supply stores) and compare those tones with the purity of neutrals (grays or white) in the original. You can correct for color casts in an original by altering tone curves for individual color channels in your scanning software (see Chapter 8).

Evaluating Sharpness

The scanning process itself causes a digitized image to lose a little of the crispness of detail it started out with. That's why higher-end scanners provide on-the-fly sharpening and why sharpening tools and filters in image-editing software were invented. But digital sharpening tools can't manufacture detail that doesn't even exist in the analog image. Make sure that the original (or at least the main subject in the original) is in relatively good focus. If the focus is slightly soft, digital sharpening tools can probably help. If the focus is hopeless, think seriously about substituting another original.

Media Considerations

A final factor to consider when evaluating artwork and documents for scanning is the source of the original. The medium in which the original was created determines at least some of the scanner settings you should use to obtain the

highest quality input possible. See Chapter 8 for detailed advice on scanning step-by-step.

> **"***Digital sharpening tools can't manufacture detail that doesn't even exist in the analog image.***"**

Reflective Originals

Originals on paper or other reflective media have an inherently narrower dynamic range than transmissive media (see Chapters 2 and 3). That range is narrowed even further after scanning, in part because scanners must rely more on reflected light to capture the colors and tones of these originals. And if the ultimate destination is print, you'll have to juggle the tonal compression issue even more deftly.

Photographic Prints

Colors on photographic prints tend to fade over time, so make sure your photographic prints are as recent a vintage as possible. Also, the original should be on glossy stock rather than matte, to avoid having the scanner amplify texture inherent in the medium. If the same image exists on both film (which has a higher density range) and print, and you have access to a scanner that can handle both, use the film as the preferred original.

Hand-Drawn Artwork

Avoid using artwork created on textured stocks, unless it's your intent to capture the grain of the paper along with the image. If the original uses a few discrete colors, consider scanning in 8-bit (rather than 24-bit) color mode to preserve the noncontinuous color look. Black-and-white hand-drawn artwork—also called *line art*—runs the risk of detail dropout if its resolution isn't high enough. Scan it either in 1-bit mode at a resolution equal to that of the final output device, or in grayscale mode (using a Gamma of 1.0 to 1.2) at no more than 1,200 ppi (see Chapter 7).

Previously Printed Visuals

Illustrators and designers occasionally need to use previously printed artwork as a basis for new artwork or as an element in a larger composition. Previously printed documents are also used frequently for OCR. The source image already has halftone patterns embedded in it, so if the digitized version needs to be printed again, there's a risk that visual interference patterns called moirés will manifest (see *Preparing Digital Images for Print*, also in the Osborne/McGraw-Hill Digital Pro series, for more information about halftoning basics and moirés). Many scanning software packages and plug-ins offer a *descreening* option that removes previous halftone patterning on the fly. If your scanner doesn't have this capability, import the digitized image into your favorite image-editing program and apply a combination of filters that first blur existing patterning and then sharpen the overall image (see Chapter 8).

Business Documents for OCR

Documents to be scanned for long-term archival should be immaculate (no coffee or food stains, please, unless you want to preserve them for posterity). If storage space is an issue, scan in 1-bit (black-and-white) mode, which yields file sizes only an eighth as large as scans in grayscale mode. The exact scanning resolution will be dictated by the final output medium—count on low resolutions (200 ppi) for documents that will be refaxed, resolutions of 600 ppi or higher for documents that will be printed later using in-house desktop printers,

and even higher resolutions for documents that will be preserved on slides or transparencies.

Transmissive Media

Transmissive media—slides, transparencies, and negative films—have long been preferred by ad agencies, marketing communications departments, and high-budget publishing concerns because their higher densities result in broader tonal ranges, and because of their inherent, first-generation sharpness. They are best scanned using high-end or desktop drum scanners, although an increasing number of flatbeds can handle them, too. Transmissive media are more subject to injuries from dust and scratches than are reflective originals, so it's vital to handle them carefully. (See the "Evaluating Physical Condition" section of this chapter.) If you're using a drum scanner, you can use transparent tape instead of oil to secure the originals to the drum, thus avoiding further risk of fingerprint or oil damage. You can also use anti-Newton spray to remove the tape after scanning.

❝Transmissive media are more subject to injuries from dust and scratches than are reflective originals.❞

Film Positives

When the artwork to be scanned is a 35mm slide or larger format transparency, avoid using duplicates as much as possible. Dupes are inherently higher in contrast than originals and risk significant loss of detail in highlights and shadows. If originals are unavailable, be prepared to tweak tonal curves extensively during or after scanning to restore a broader tonal range.

Film Negatives

Not all scanners can digitize negative film, for reasons discussed in Chapter 3. If yours can, investigate the software options and make sure that the scanner does more than just invert the colors of the negatives. You may need to compensate for inherent color cast of the film's substrate or base either on the fly during scanning or later, using an image-editing program.

The more thoroughly you can quality-control source images prior to scanning them, the easier it becomes to avoid the "garbage in, garbage out" syndrome. Since compensating for flaws as a post-processing task is more time consuming than when you weed them out beforehand, your scanning productivity will also improve.

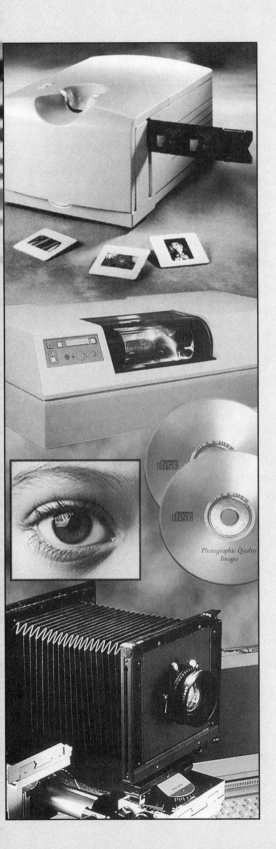

7

Resolution and Sizing

The issues of resolution and sizing generate more confusion than almost any other subject related to scanning and input. What role does resolution play in digital images? What input resolution should you choose when scanning an original? How much resolution is enough to guarantee high-quality output, and is there such a thing as too much? When is it acceptable to resize an image, and what's the best method for doing so? And what in the world *is* resolution, anyway?

In this chapter, we'll provide answers to all of these questions and more. We'll examine each of the following topics, suggesting practical guidelines that will help you maintain the highest possible image quality from input to final output:

- Resolution and its relationship to basic attributes of pixels
- Determining the optimum scanning or input resolution for your final output goals
- How resolution affects image quality, file size, ease of manipulation, file transfer time, and cost of output

- How halftoning conventions used in printing determine both input and output resolution
- Resizing and resampling digital images to avoid degradation

Just What *Is* Resolution, Anyway?

We've already stated once that if terms in the digital imaging field were actors, resolution would win an Oscar for versatility, but it bears repeating here. Whatever its costume or role, though, the most basic fact about resolution is that it always concerns either the *amount* or *density* of digital information. Any discussion of resolution must therefore be inextricably linked to the properties of pixels and grids, which are essential components of the raster images that both scanners and output devices reproduce. Let's examine the attributes of pixels to place resolution in the context of the "big picture" of digital imaging.

The Attributes of Pixels

An original grayscale or color photograph has *continuous tone*—there's a smooth transition between adjacent colors or shades. Computers, on the other hand, can't understand anything continuous; information has to be broken down into discrete units for it to be digestible. The pixel, or *picture element*, is the smallest unit by which image data can be measured. And the challenge of all digital image reproduction is to simulate continuous tones using these small, noncontinuous individual elements.

Every pixel in a raster image has four basic properties—size, tonal value, color depth, and location. All four of these attributes help define resolution, each in a different way.

Pixel Size

All pixels within the same image have a uniform size. Initially, pixel size is determined by the resolution at which an image is scanned or digitally captured. A scanning resolution of 600 ppi, for example, indicates that each pixel is only $1/600$ inch. Higher input resolutions generate smaller pixels, which in turn mean more information and potential detail per unit of measurement and a more continuous-tone appearance. Lower resolutions mean larger pixels, less detail per unit of measurement, and a more jagged appearance. Together, the size and number of pixels in an image determine the total amount of information it contains. You can change pixel size at any point in the production process by changing the resolution; if you'll be outputting to print, altering the resolution automatically changes the print dimensions.

Color or Tonal Value

Scanners and filmless cameras assign a single color or gray value to each pixel in an image. The illusion of continuous tone comes about when pixels are small *and* when adjacent pixels vary only slightly from one another in color or tone. Images scanned using devices that have a low noise factor and broad dynamic range appear most naturally continuous in tone because they include an especially broad range of tones from light to dark.

Tip: Detail in an image is a function of both pixel size and tonal range. Pixel size relates directly to resolution, while tonal range is determined by the dynamic range of the scanning device.

Color Depth

Granted, a single pixel can have only one value assigned to it, but it's the bit depth or color depth of the digitizing device that determines how many *potential* colors or tones are available to assign. Every additional bit demands more file storage space, even as it increases the smoothness of transitions between adjacent colors and tones (see Figure C–1 in the color gallery).

Pixel Location

A raster image is nothing more than a grid of discrete pixels, each of which has a definable horizontal and vertical position within the grid. In most major image-editing programs, you can obtain the coordinates of any pixel by moving an Eyedropper tool over it. The physical size of the grid, determined by the total number of pixels and by resolution, determines the relative position of pixels.

The Many Faces of Resolution

Depending on your workflow, you may have to contend with several different types of resolution: input (scanning), optical, interpolated, monitor, image, output, and printer resolution. These seemingly confusing usages have a common denominator—they're all concerned with the amount or density of digital information. The variables have to do with either the type of device being used to measure this density or the stage of the production process at which it's being measured—refer to the following glossary-in-a-nutshell.

- *Input* or *scanning resolution* refers to the amount of information that a flatbed, transparency, or drum scanner captures per inch or centimeter of an original. Input resolution can vary every time you scan. It's limited only by the maximum optical or interpolated resolution of which a particular scanning device is capable.

- *Optical resolution* describes the *maximum* amount or density of information that the optical system of a scanner or filmless camera can sample (per horizontal inch or centimeter for scanners, or expressed as a fixed amount for filmless cameras).

- *Interpolated resolution* can apply to either the input or output phase of the production process. In the context of input, interpolated resolution describes the maximum density of information that a scanner can simulate with the help of firmware or software algorithms. If a previously digitized image that you're preparing for output doesn't contain enough information to print well, you can also interpolate its resolution, adding new pixels to increase resolution, dimensions, or both. Interpolation always compromises image integrity, so avoid it in both input and output whenever possible.

- *Image resolution* defines the total amount of information in a digital image at any stage during the production process and is expressed in pixels (512×768, for example). Photo CD images, which have already been scanned by the time you receive them, are available for downloading in five or six different image resolutions. Image resolution is also important for determining whether an image contains the right amount of information to output well, whatever the medium.

- *Monitor (display) resolution* describes either the total amount of information that a computer screen can display at one time (1024×768 pixels, for example) or the number of dots per horizontal inch of the monitor (such as 72 dpi). Display resolution affects only the end user's convenience when working with images, not the output quality of the image data.

- *Output resolution* applies to print projects only and expresses the number of pixels per inch (ppi or dpi) at which a final image file needs to be sent to an imagesetter or printer. Together, the print reproduction method, the conventions of halftoning, and the resolution of the chosen output device determine the correct output resolution for images in a given project (see "Halftoning Basics" later in this chapter). If you know the desired output resolution, halftone screen frequency, print dimensions, and original dimensions in advance, you can derive the correct scanning resolution for an original.

- *Printer resolution* measures the number of horizontal and vertical dots per inch that an output device can generate. The higher a printer's or imagesetter's resolution, the smaller the dots it can create, and the more continuous in tone the resulting images appear to be. Printer resolution limits the maximum number of discrete tones that can be reproduced in print.

Resolution Quality Control

With so many different types of resolution to juggle, you might be wondering which ones are the most important to control. Actually, the issue is pretty straightforward. To ensure image quality from input all the way to output, you need to coordinate only two types of resolution if you're outputting to slide, multimedia, or video, and four types if you're outputting to print:

- **Input resolution**—Make certain that enough information gets into the digitized image to meet the requirements of the desired final product.

- **Image resolution**—Verify that the image contains neither too little nor too much information for good output results.

- **Printer resolution** (print output)—Determine the maximum resolution of which the printer is capable, which in turn determines the halftone screen frequency (for PostScript devices) that will produce the smoothest gradation of tones.

- **Output resolution** (print output)—Ensure that the density of information meets the requirements of the halftone screen frequency (for imagesetters and PostScript printers) or equals the resolution of the printer (for continuous-tone printers).

If you can obtain as much information as possible about the output requirements for your project in advance, you can eliminate guesswork about scanning resolution. The next section of this chapter guides you through the process of coordinating these types of resolution to select the best possible input resolution for any job.

Determining an Optimum Scanning Resolution

Resolution is not the only factor determining the quality of a scan; equally important are the input device's signal-to-noise ratio and dynamic range, which define the purity of tones and the clarity of detail (see Chapter 2). Yet resolution—if it's handled correctly—contributes significantly to the perception of detail by providing the right amount and density of information to simulate continuous tonality. Correctly chosen resolution also helps ensure that tones in a digitized image remain faithful to the original.

Many users of scanning products take a willy-nilly approach to input resolution, arbitrarily scanning at the highest resolution the device can support, or using some magic number they've "heard" is the universally correct one. In some cases, users assume that it's OK to send the image for output "as is," regardless of the amount of information it contains. This fatal mistake can lead to apparent "jaggies" when the image doesn't contain enough information, or to loss of image contrast and unnecessarily higher output cost when the image contains too much (see "Screen Angles and the Halftoning Factor: How

Much Resolution Is Enough?" later in this chapter). Just as frequently, the assumption is made that it's OK to blithely jettison any excess information or to add extra information through resampling later on. What these users don't realize is that whenever data is added to or subtracted from an image, there's a loss. The loss may affect sharpness, contrast, tonal range, or all of the above (see "Resizing and Resampling Images" later in this chapter). Although it's possible to do a certain amount of damage control after the fact to compensate for unwise decisions made during scanning, the ideal situation is to choose the optimum input resolution up front.

There's no universally "correct" input resolution that applies to all images. The goal is to obtain exactly the right amount of *information* to meet your output needs, which you can calculate if you first answer these few basic questions about your project:

- What are the dimensions of the original? If you plan to scan only a portion of the original, enter the cropped dimensions into the scanner interface.

- To what medium will you output the image—print, computer-based multimedia or presentations, video, or film recorder?

- What are the final output dimensions? If you're outputting to print, the dimensions can vary from one image to the next. Other output media have fixed dimensions, which streamline your decisions about how much information to include in an image.

- If your output will be to print media, is the final output device a halftone printer or a continuous-tone printer, and what is the printer's resolution? If you're using a halftone device, what screen frequency will you be assigning for the project?

- What will be the bit depth of the scanned image—line art (1-bit), grayscale (8-bit), or color (24-bit)?

Armed with the foregoing information, you have all the knowledge you need to determine an input resolution that will exactly match your quality-control requirements for both image resolution and output resolution. Let's first look at some general technological and practical guidelines that should govern all your resolution decisions, and then move on to the section that's appropriate for your chosen output medium.

Tip: *If you use Photo CD images in your projects, let Kodak's Beacon application (provided on newer Photo CDs) automatically calculate the correct Image Pac resolution to download.*

Making the Most of a Scanner's Capabilities

Every scanning device has resolution limits. You'll produce the best images by working within those limits rather than against them. Ideally, you should scan at 100 percent magnification using an input resolution that's evenly divisible by your scanner's optical resolution. In the print publishing world, where original sizes and output sizes vary greatly, it's critical that you develop a system for calculating scanning resolution that allows for resizing. But whatever your output medium, observing the following rules as often as possible will deliver the best tonal fidelity relative to your originals.

Avoid Interpolation

Don't scan at resolutions higher than the scanning device's maximum optical resolution. At interpolated resolutions, scanners use firmware- or software-based algorithms to add new data to an image. Although some algorithms are better than others, you never gain new detail through interpolation, and you can actually degrade sharpness and contrast due to the way pixel values are averaged. If your in-house scanner can't cut the mustard at the optical resolution you need, send out for a higher-resolution scan or buy a scanner with better capabilities.

Marketing hype sometimes makes it tricky to determine just what a scanner's maximum optical resolution is. If a scanner manufacturer advertises a horizontal resolution that's lower than the vertical resolution—600 × 1200 or 400 × 800 ppi, for example—you can usually assume that the "true" optical resolution is limited to the lower of the two numbers, which represents the actual number of sensor elements in the linear CCD (charge-coupled device) array. So, to avoid compromising color or grayscale values when using a 600 × 1200-ppi scanner, you'd do well to scan at a maximum resolution of 600 × 600 ppi.

Tip: *There are exceptions to this rule. Scanning at interpolated resolutions probably won't subvert your purposes if you plan to use the original artwork as a template, a basis for digital painting, filtering, extensive manipulation, or as the source for a texture.*

Scan at Integral Resolutions

Engineers admonish us to scan at resolutions that are evenly divisible by a scanner's optical resolution—600 ppi, 300 ppi, 200 ppi, 150 ppi, 100 ppi, or 75 ppi for a 600-ppi scanner, for example. The reason for recommending these *integral scanning* resolutions is simple. If you choose some other input resolution, a scanner has to play math games when determining color or grayscale values for a given pixel, and averaging will take place that compromises the tonal integrity of the original.

What if the use of an integral scanning resolution generates less information than you need? A good rule of thumb in these cases is to scan at the next highest integral resolution and then to *downsample* the image (subtracting pixels) as a post-processing step. Although

you'll still incur some compromises through averaging, the downsampled image will provide all the information that the output device can use to build its halftone or continuous-tone product. Any excess information provided will either be discarded or averaged, softening the detail.

Scan at Integral Enlargement Factors

Many scanning experts recommend the use of integral enlargement factors for the same reason that they recommend integral scanning resolutions—to avoid compromising the capabilities of a scanner's optical system. For best results, scan at 100 percent, 200 percent, 300 percent, and so forth of the original size, up to (but not beyond) the scanner's maximum optical resolution. If a particular integral enlargement factor doesn't yield an adequate amount of information, select the next highest enlargement factor and then downsample the image later as a post-processing step.

How Resolution Affects Workflow

From a purely practical standpoint, the resolution you choose when scanning an image has consequences for the rest of your workflow cycle. Input resolution affects the file size of an image, the ease and speed with which you manipulate it, the amount of time needed to transfer files to and from clients or vendors, and the cost of output. These are strong arguments for putting your scanner on a diet and making sure you don't scan in more information than you actually need.

Resolution and File Size

These days, most scanning software applications automatically calculate file size for you according to the way you crop the preview of the original and the color mode and input resolution you select (Figure 7–1). If necessary, though, you can estimate file size manually if you know the horizontal and vertical dimensions of the original, the color mode, and the intended input resolution. Table 7–1, located at the end of this chapter, contains handy formulas for calculating enlargement factor, file size, scanning resolution, and other job parameters in advance of scanning.

Scanning resolution has a geometric relationship to file size, not a linear one as with color mode (see Chapter 5). Let's say you're planning to scan a three-inch square original in RGB mode. If you choose an input resolution of 300 ppi, you'll generate an image with a file size of approximately 2.4MB, as shown by this sample equation (see Table 7–1):

$$[3 \text{ in.} \times 3 \text{ in.} \times (300 \text{ ppi})^2 \times 3] \div 1,000 = 2.43\text{MB}$$

If you scan the image again, doubling the scanning resolution to 600 ppi, you'll *quadruple* the file size:

$$[3 \text{ in.} \times 3 \text{ in.} \times (600 \text{ ppi})^2 \times 3] \div 1,000 = 9.72\text{MB}$$

Tripling the input resolution would result in a file nine times larger than the original, quadrupling it would generate a file sixteen times larger, and so on. If you generate more information than you need for quality output, you're lugging around a lot of dead weight.

Once scanning has been completed, changing the resolution of an image alters only its physical size; the file size remains constant unless you use resampling to subtract from or add to the amount of

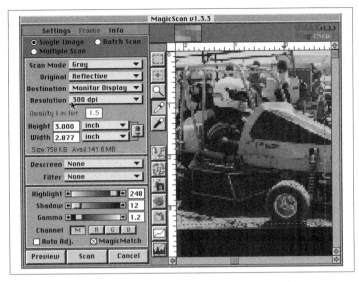

Figure 7–1

Scanning software typically calculates file size automatically based on the input resolution, color mode, quality factor, and cropping dimensions you specify. The UMAX MagicScan plug-in for Adobe Photoshop, shown above, bases file size on the Resolution, Quality Factor, Height, and Width fields.

information in the image (see "Resizing and Resampling Images"). That's why a low-resolution image with large dimensions may have a file size no greater than that of a small image at high resolution.

Image Manipulation, Storage, File Transfer Time

Scanning images at a higher resolution than necessary takes its toll on your precious time and also hogs valuable system resources such as RAM and storage space. Unless you use HSC Live Picture or Fauve Xres, images that contain too much information require more time to complete each operation in an image-editing program. Multiply that extra time by the number of operations in a typical image preparation session, and you begin to glean the consequences of digital waste. Excessively large file sizes also require more RAM during manipulation, more hard drive or removable drive space for storage, and more time to transfer images to colleagues or to an offsite designer, service bureau, color house, or client.

Cost of Output

Many service bureaus, color prepress houses, slide output and video production services, and quick printers charge for output based on processing time, as well as number of pieces. Files that contain an excessive amount of information naturally take longer to process, and guess who foots the bill?

Determining how much information you need for output is simple when the output medium is one that requires a fixed amount of information (as is the case with presentations, multimedia, or film recorders). Figuring this out is more difficult for print media, where variable output sizing, screening technologies, and halftoning factors enter into the picture. See the section "Screen Angles and the Halftoning Factor: How Much Resolution Is Enough?" later in this chapter for more detailed guidelines.

Scanning Resolution for Print Output

Service bureaus, color prepress houses, and full-service or quick print shops frequently complain that a majority of customer-scanned image files arrive for output containing *too much* information rather than too little. Although you may not realize it, there's a strong possibility that you or your workgroup colleagues are generating image files the size of the state of Texas, when files as small as Rhode Island would do the job equally well. You owe it to your budget (and your schedule!) to memorize the next few pages.

To determine an appropriate scanning resolution for any original that's destined for print, it's essential to know the physical dimensions of the original and the desired dimensions of the final image in the printed document. These two pieces of information allow you to calculate the *enlargement* or *scale factor*—the number of times that an original must be enlarged or

reduced during scanning (see Table 7–1). Beyond that, you need to know a few things about the final output device—not the device you'll be using for proof prints, but the one that yields the final or plate-ready output. If the final output device is a halftoning device (PostScript printer, imagesetter, or platemaker), you should know the resolution at which you will print, the halftone screen frequency that you will specify for output, and the type of screening technology that will be used for the job (see the "Halftoning Basics" section later in this chapter). If you're using a continuous-tone printer, knowing the printer's resolution will help you calculate the correct resolution to use when scanning. Finally, the bit depth at which you scan also impacts the resolution at which the image should be output. The output resolution of bitmaps (black-and-white line art) needs to match the resolution of the final printing device as closely as possible, which is not the case with grayscale and color images. As always, the best way to ensure that an image will have sufficient output resolution is to plan for it during the input stage.

> **❝Service bureaus frequently complain that customer-scanned image files contain more data than necessary.❞**

Scanning Resolution for Output to Halftoning Devices

PostScript printing devices such as black-and-white or color laser printers, imagesetters, and platesetters simulate continuous tones by varying the sizes of dots (see "Halftoning Basics" later in this chapter). If your final output is to a halftoning device, you'll need to take both the printer resolution and the halftone screen frequency into consideration when calculating scanning resolution. The printer resolution must be high enough to support the desired screen frequency, or you'll have to compromise between contrast and detail. The type of screening technology you're using for output is also a factor in determining how much information the scanned image must contain.

Halftoning output using conventional screening technologies

The conventional halftone screening technologies used by most PostScript printing devices generate variably sized dots in fixed locations and rotate the screens for each color plate at a given angle. These screen angles affect the amount of information necessary to produce accurate halftone dots, expressed as a *halftoning factor* or *quality factor* that needs to be taken into account when calculating input resolution or output resolution (see the section "Screen Angles and the Halftoning Factor: How Much Resolution Is Enough?" later in this chapter). There's considerable debate in the industry about what number to use as the halftoning factor; we feel that "less is more" and so we use 1.5. If your final images will be grayscale or color, use this formula (also listed in Table 7–1) to determine an appropriate scanning resolution for originals that will be output to halftoning devices using conventional screening technologies:

```
Scanning resolution = Enlargement factor
      × 1.5 × Halftone screen frequency
```

Halftoning output using FM screening technologies

Recently developed screening technologies, collectively referred to as *FM* or *frequency-modulated* screening, create output using irregular patterns of variably shaped dots rather than regular patterns of fixed size dots. Since FM screening software runs primarily on PostScript halftoning devices, you still have to concern yourself with a nominal screen frequency, but the halftoning factor reduces to somewhere between 1.0 and 1.2 because there are no screen angles to compensate for (see "Stochastic and Frequency-Modulated (FM) Screening" later in this chapter). Use the following formula to derive the optimum scanning resolution for color and grayscale images that will be output using FM screening technologies:

```
Scanning resolution = Enlargement factor × 1
      × Halftone screen frequency
```

Scanning Resolution for Continuous-Tone Printer Output

Not all printers use halftoning or FM screening. Dye sublimation printers, liquid and solid ink-jet printers, color copiers, and some thermal wax printers are called *continuous-tone printers* because they blend pigments directly to produce smooth, continuous-tone output. When calculating scanning resolution for originals for which continuous-tone printers will be the final output device, you need consider only the enlargement factor and the printer resolution:

```
Scanning resolution = Enlargement factor
      × Printer resolution
```

The foregoing formula assumes that the output resolution of the image needs to be identical to the printer resolution. Some industry professionals, though, are of the opinion that an output resolution equal to only 75 percent of a continuous-tone printer's resolution (for example, 225 ppi output for a 300 dpi dye sublimation printer) yields acceptable quality output. If you or your service bureau finds this lower resolution workable, multiply the enlargement factor by .75 to obtain the best scanning resolution for the original. (Use the next highest integral resolution if the number you arrive at isn't exactly divisible by the scanner's optical resolution.)

Scanning Resolution for Line Art

When you scan an original in line art mode, all pixels in the resulting image are either black or white. Line art scanning is appropriate for reproducing logos, abstract designs, and pen-and-ink technical illustrations.

Scanning line art can be tricky because of the difficulty of exactly aligning pixels in the scanned image with the edges of fine lines or shapes in the original. Jaggies become apparent wherever lines or shapes aren't divisible by an even number of pixels. Printing line art is equally tricky, for the same reason: pixels may not align precisely with the printer dots and spots laid down by the output device.

Using higher scanning and output resolutions than are typical for continuous-tone images can solve many of the problems associated with reproducing line art.

- Scan the original at a high resolution. Higher scanning resolutions translate to smaller pixels and, consequently, to smoother lines and shapes.

- Make sure that at the desired print dimensions, the output resolution of the line art image is equal to the resolution of the printer, at least at printer resolutions of up to 1,200 dpi. (Output resolutions above 1,200 dpi don't seem to make much visible difference.)

Tip: *Line art presents one rare exception to the rule about not using interpolation when scanning images. Since you're not working with continuous tones, adding pixels through interpolation can smooth the image and reinforce detail at the same time.*

Use this formula to ensure that a line art image will contain enough information to print well:

```
Scanning resolution = Enlargement factor
                    × Printer resolution
```

Figure 7–2 shows examples of black-and-white clip art scanned at various resolutions and then output to an imagesetter at 2,400 dpi. Note how detail increases and the jaggies diminish as image resolution increases. Chapter 8 includes additional tips for generating high-quality line art scans.

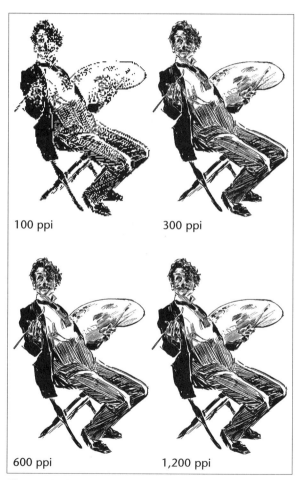

100 ppi   300 ppi

600 ppi   1,200 ppi

Figure 7–2

Smoothness of detail in scanned line art increases as the output resolution approaches the resolution of the final output device. Output resolutions above 1,200 ppi, though, don't create a noticeable improvement in image quality.

Scanning Resolution for Computer-Based Multimedia and Presentations

It's relatively easy to figure out an appropriate scanning resolution for originals that will be output to computer-based multimedia and presentations, because the amount of information that computer monitors support is fixed. So is the *aspect ratio* of monitors, which is the numerical relationship between width and height. The fixed aspect ratio of the output medium means that depending on the format of the original, you may need to crop it horizontally or vertically either during or after scanning to make it fit. Here's the formula for determining scanning resolution for monitor-based output:

```
Scanning resolution = Vertical monitor
resolution (in pixels) ÷ Narrowest dimension
of original
```

So, for example, scanning a 5 × 7-inch glossy print for use in a presentation projected from a 1,024 × 768 monitor would require an input resolution of approximately 154 ppi (768 ÷ 5 = 153.6). Uncropped, the original would yield a file containing 1,024 × 768 pixels, just slightly wider than the monitor dimensions and needing to be cropped horizontally. Of course, if you intend to use an original as only one small component of the output screen, the input resolution can be much lower.

Scanning Resolution for Video Output

Standard NTSC video produces an analog signal that's equivalent to 525 × 486 pixels of information. If you're scanning a still image for video output, however, it's a good idea to increase the horizontal and vertical graymap dimensions of the base image to about 10 percent beyond the area of interest. This practice allows for the 10 percent overscan phenomenon known as the *NTSC safe area*.

The aspect ratio and amount of information in an analog video image, like the aspect ratio and amount of information on a computer monitor, are fixed. Chances are that the originals you scan won't have the same aspect ratio as the video signal, so cropping could be necessary. Use this formula to obtain an optimum scanning resolution, taking care to include the overscan information in the vertical dimension of the video frame:

```
Scanning resolution = Vertical dimension of
video frame, in pixels ÷ Narrowest dimension
of original
```

Analog video isn't the only game in town these days. There are also all-digital video formats for use in computer-based training and entertainment. The most common digital video format is 322 × 240 pixels, although higher-resolution formats such as 640 × 480 and 686 × 486 are also in use. The safe area doesn't apply to digital video, so you don't need to scan extra information into the base image.

Tip: Always edit images intended for North American video output on an NTSC-compatible monitor to ensure that you'll be seeing the colors that will actually appear in video.

Scanning Resolution for Film Recorder Output

Slides and transparencies remain a popular, portable form of output for illustrators, photographers, and designers. The amount of digital information that film recorders can accept is fixed and depends on the film format used. Film format also determines the aspect ratio of the final slide or transparency.

Film recorders measure output resolution in terms of *lines*, which measures the number of pixels along the broadest dimension of the film.

Film recorders that use 35mm film, for example, typically image slides at 8,000 (8,192), 4,000 (4,096) or 2,000 (2,048) lines. Since 35mm slides have a 3:2 aspect ratio, you can easily determine that an image intended for 4,000-line output should contain 4,096 × 2,727 pixels of information, while an image intended for 2,000-line output would contain 2,048 × 1,363 pixels of information. Film recorders can also rotate images by 90 degrees to accommodate vertical or horizontal formats as required. Once you know the output film format and the dimensions of the original, use these formulas to determine the best scanning resolution:

```
Scanning resolution, horizontal-format originals
= Width of broadest dimension of output media,
        in pixels ÷ Width of original

Scanning resolution, vertical-format originals =
Width of broadest dimension of output media, in
        pixels ÷ Height of original
```

As with images intended for computer monitor or video output, cropping may be necessary during or after scanning to force the aspect ratio of the digital image to fit the output format.

Scanning Resolution When Output Size Is Unknown

Under some circumstances—when you're scanning for an unknown output medium or for multiple types of output, or when the designer hasn't told you the final print dimensions—it's just not possible to determine a precise scanning resolution or the exact amount of information an image must contain. Here's the best approach to take in such cases:

1. Estimate the largest output size you are likely to require.

2. Scan at a resolution that will yield enough information for good output at this estimated largest size. Be sure to use an integral scanning resolution!

3. When output time rolls around and you finally have all the output specifications in hand, downsample the file as required. (See the "Resizing and Resampling Images" section of this chapter.)

Tip: *Another approach is to first scan the image at 72 dpi for position only, allow the designer to manipulate the image for layout as desired, and then rescan the image at the appropriate resolution once the final size is known.*

Halftoning Basics

Commercial printing presses can't reproduce continuous-tone artwork directly. Instead, they use a process called *halftoning* to simulate the look of continuous tones. Basically, halftoning involves the use of variably sized dots to generate different shades of an ink color, with larger dots representing darker shades and smaller dots representing lighter ones. A 30 percent gray, for example, is created not with 30 percent gray ink, but with black ink that covers only 30 percent of the surface area assigned to that shade (Figure 7–3).

Halftoning has two aspects that are relevant to resolution and important for you to understand if you scan images for print. These aspects are screen frequency, which affects the tonal range and level of detail that are possible in the final output, and screen angle, which affects the amount of information that a scanned image must contain in order to output well.

Spots and Dots: Halftone Cells, Screen Frequency, and Detail

There's a difference between halftoning as the printing industry practiced it traditionally and the way it's been handled since the introduction of computer-based publishing. In traditional

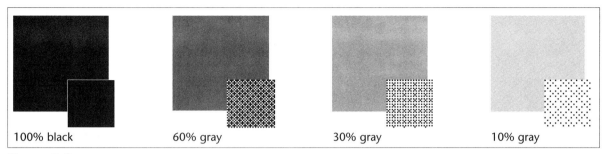

100% black   60% gray   30% gray   10% gray

Figure 7–3

Through halftoning, a single ink color can reproduce a broad range of tones, varying the size of ink dots on the page to express the various tones found in an image.

halftoning, printers photographed continuous-tone art through a heavy-gauge, flexible film contact screen that broke down the tones of the original into variably sized *halftone dots*. However, digital halftoning devices—imagesetters, digital platesetters, color and black-and-white laser printers, color thermal wax transfer printers—can create only fixed-size dots (let's call them *spots* to avoid confusing them with halftone dots). To reproduce the variably sized halftone dots of traditional halftoning, these PostScript-based printing devices group fixed-size spots together in a matrix called a *halftone cell* (Figure 7–4). The dot in each halftone cell reproduces exactly one shade of gray (or of a process ink color). The density of that shade and the size of the

halftone dot are directly related to the number of fixed-size spots in each halftone cell, which in turn is determined by the numeric value (0 to 255) assessed for each pixel.

We refer to the number of halftone dots per linear inch in a printed image as the *halftone screen frequency* or *line screen*. Screen frequency, expressed in *lpi* (lines per inch), has a great deal to do with the amount of detail that can be reproduced in print. If the screen frequency is low—if a printed image contains only a few halftone dots per linear inch—only a limited amount of detail will be apparent. As the line screen increases, more detail can be reproduced. Figure 7–5 demonstrates this principle showing a grayscale image printed at several different halftone screen frequency settings.

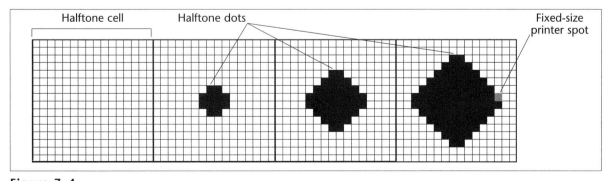

Halftone cell   Halftone dots   Fixed-size printer spot

Figure 7–4

As the number of fixed-size printer spots in a digital halftone cell increases, so does the apparent density or darkness of the tone.

20 lpi

60 lpi

85 lpi

133 lpi

Figure 7–5   © Emil Ihrig

The amount of detail that can be reproduced by a halftoning output device is determined by the halftone screen frequency, or number of halftone dots per linear inch. The tonal range, on the other hand, is determined by a trade-off between line screen and printer resolution. These samples were output on a high-resolution imagesetter, which at 2,540 dpi contains enough resolution to reproduce the full tonal range (256 shades of gray) that PostScript supports. At the lower halftone screen frequencies, however, not enough detail is available to simulate a continuous-tone look. Figure C–12 in the color gallery shows the same principle at work with full-color images.

Note: *Higher lpi doesn't improve poor quality originals, it merely exposes them. The quality of the detail in the digital image limits the detail delivered by any halftone.*

Tonal Range: Balancing Printer Resolution and Screen Frequency

So far, so good. Just crank up the halftone screen frequency infinitely and you'll be able to obtain continuous-tone photographic detail from a 300 dpi laser printer, right? Not

quite. There are two factors that contribute to a halftone printing device's ability to simulate continuous tones. One factor is detail, the other is *tonal range*—the number of discrete tones that can be expressed accurately between solid black and paper white. As you've already seen, halftone screen frequency controls the level of detail, but it's the relationship between screen frequency and printer resolution that determines the tonal range.

Ideally, a printed grayscale image should be able to reproduce 256 shades of gray, and a full-color image should be able to reproduce 256 shades for each of the process ink colors. However, the number of possible shades that a halftone cell can reproduce is limited by the resolution of the printing device. In fact, the relationship between printer resolution and halftone screen frequency is an inverse one. Here's how to calculate the maximum number of shades per color that a given printing device can reproduce (also refer to Table 7–1):

```
(Printer resolution ÷ Halftone
    screen frequency)² + 1
= Max. number of tonal levels
```

You can understand why digital halftoning works this way if you recall that a printer's linear resolution is fixed. As you cram additional halftone dots into each linear inch, fewer spots are available to each horizontal grid line in a halftone cell. As the line screen increases, the number of potential gray shades that each halftone cell can reproduce decreases geometrically. A 300 dpi laser printer, for example, can reproduce no more than 33 shades of gray at a line screen of 53 lpi ($[300 \div 53]^2 + 1$ = approximately 33). If you crank up the line screen to 75 lpi, you get more detail, but the image is higher in contrast because it can't express as many discrete tones ($[300 \div 75]^2 + 1 = 17$). By the same reasoning, a 600 dpi printer can reproduce 65 tones at a line screen of 75 lpi, and a 1,200 dpi printer or imagesetter can reproduce 178 tones at a line screen of 90 lpi. An imagesetter or platesetter printing at 2,400 dpi can reproduce the full range of 256 tones per color at line screens of up to 150 lpi.

Screen Angles and the Halftoning Factor: How Much Resolution Is Enough?

The interfaces of some flatbed, slide, and drum scanners ask you to enter a *halftoning factor* or *quality factor* as one of the bases for determining input resolution. These terms, which apply only to scans destined for print output, address the issue of how many pixels worth of information are necessary to accurately determine the tonal value in one halftone dot. Some professionals say the ratio should be 2:1, while others claim that a 1.5:1 ratio serves the purpose.

At some time during your scanning career, you've probably heard the dictum, "Output resolution should be twice the halftone screen frequency in order to produce an accurate halftone dot." Nobody really knows where this rule came from, but most of us follow it like lemmings to the sea. Trouble is, you don't really need that much information in an image. Blind adherence to the 2:1 output resolution-to-screen-frequency ratio has a negative impact on both the budget and the quality of the printed image. It leads to oversized files that cost too much to output and, more important, to a flattening of image contrast. These days, a growing number of prepress professionals are of the opinion that a

resolution-to-screen-frequency ratio of only 1.5:1 delivers all the information that's really required to produce good halftone dots (see Figure C–13 in the color insert). Let's examine why a ratio other than 1:1 is necessary and why a resolution-to-screen-frequency ratio of 1.5:1 (or thereabouts) makes sense.

Tip: Remember, output resolution describes the density of information in a digital image at the time it's sent to a printer or imagesetter. It's different from scanning resolution, which has to take enlargement (scaling) factors and the size of the original into account.

Halftone screen angles are at the heart of the resolution-to-screen-frequency ratio controversy. Scanning resolution is always measured at a horizontal angle of zero degrees. But when an imagesetter, platesetter, or other PostScript printing device generates digital halftones or color separations, the halftone screen or screens are rotated at an angle so that the observer's eye doesn't perceive the screen patterning. In grayscale images, which have only one color (black), the screen is rotated at 45 degrees. In full-color CMYK images, typical screen angles are 105 degrees for the cyan plate, 75 degrees for magenta, 90 degrees for yellow, and 45 degrees for black. (Various imagesetter manufacturers have created their own proprietary angling schemes, but you needn't worry about that here.) Using a different angle for each color screen prevents the muddying that would occur if all ink colors were directly overprinted on top of each other. For our purposes, the most important thing to remember is that of the four CMYK screen angles, the 45-degree angle of the black plate represents the widest angle relative to a horizontal line.

Note: The downside of screen angles is that if they are not placed at the precisely correct angles as they address one another, annoyingly visible moiré patterns will develop in the printed image.

This discrepancy between the perfectly horizontal angle of scanning resolution and the angles of halftone screens is important because it impacts the amount of information necessary to build each halftone dot in PostScript. Theoretically, a single pixel should provide all the information necessary to generate one halftone dot—a perfect 1:1 ratio. In practice, this doesn't happen because when you rotate a horizontal line of a given length by 45 degrees, the *horizontal* real estate it covers is greatly diminished (see Figure 7–6). To compensate for that apparent "shortening," you'd have to extend the horizontal line by 1.41 times its original length, equaling the length of the diagonal line. Note also that in the halftone diagram in Figure 7–7, a right triangle is formed by the horizontal line (*B*, the scanner CCD array), the vertical line (*A*, scanner CCD travel), and the diagonal line (*C*, the direction of the halftone dot). Remember the $A^2 + B^2 = C^2$ right triangle

geometry equation you learned in high school? That's just another way of saying that the diagonal line—the line that represents the halftone screen angle—is 1.41 times longer than either the horizontal or the vertical line.

What this means is that the raster image processor (RIP) of a PostScript halftoning device requires the equivalent of only about 1.41 pixels of data to produce one accurate halftone dot—not two pixels as is often assumed. (The ratios would be even lower than 1.4:1 for the cyan, magenta, and yellow angles, but 1.41:1 takes care of the worst-case scenario black angle.) The scanning utility ScanPrepPro from ImageXpress uses this ratio to calculate the precise scanning resolution automatically, or to resample a previously scanned image (Figure 7–7).

The case becomes even clearer when you recognize that an RIP averages *all* the tonal values within each halftone cell area to arrive at a single number from which it can produce one

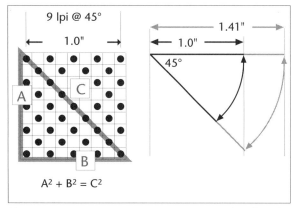

Figure 7–6

courtesy ImageXpress, Inc.

*Why a 1.41:1 output resolution-to-screen-frequency ratio makes sense. Rotating a horizontal line by 45 degrees, as in the halftone screen of the black printing plate (**left**), results in an apparent "shortening" of the horizontal area covered by the line (**right**). Increasing the length of the line by a factor of 1.41 compensates for this shortening effect. High school geometry shows that the 45-degree angle of the black plate (the widest CMYK angle relative to the horizontal plane) generates a line 1.41 times longer than the horizontal line that represents the angle of scanning.*

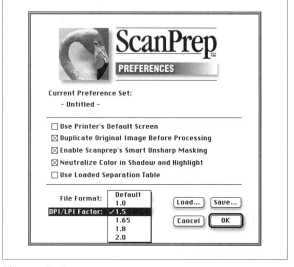

Figure 7–7

ScanPrepPro's ScanPrep Calculator uses a default resolution-to-screen-frequency ratio of 1.41 to calculate correct input resolution (or output resolution for previously scanned images). Users can override this setting and determine their own ratio up to 2:1.

halftone dot. Figure 7–8 shows that if an image contains much more information than necessary (2:1 output resolution-to-screen-frequency ratio), then the RIP ends up averaging multiple color or grayscale values and reducing them to a single value, with unfortunate consequences for image contrast and detail.

Let's do an example calculation to show the consequences of being a digital pack rat with regard to scanning resolution. Assume you're scanning an 8 × 10-inch color original that will be printed at 4 × 5 inches (a .5 enlargement factor) using a halftone screen frequency of 150 lpi. If you scan the original based on a 2:1 halftoning factor so that the final image will contain twice as many pixels per inch as lines per inch in the final halftone, you'll end up with a file size of 5.4MB (see Table 7–1):

```
Scanning resolution = 0.5 (enlargement factor) × 2
(halftoning factor) × 150 (screen frequency) = 150 ppi

File size = 8 in. (horizontal) × 10 in. (vertical)
            × (150 ppi)² × 3 = 5.4MB
```

Now, let's assume a 1.5:1 resolution-to-screen-frequency ratio—granted, 1.41 isn't the most convenient number to remember, so we'll substitute 1.5 for the sake of simplicity. The scanning resolution decreases, the file shrinks to a much more economical size, and there's less likelihood of compromise to image detail and contrast:

```
Scanning resolution = 0.5 (enlargement factor) × 1.5
(halftoning factor) × 150 (screen frequency) = 112.5 ppi

File size = 8 in. (horizontal)×10 in. (vertical)
            × (112.5 ppi)² × 3 = 3.0MB
```

Tip: *When a 1.5:1 resolution-to-screen-frequency ratio doesn't result in an integral scanning resolution, use the next highest integral scanning resolution (such as 150 ppi) and then downsample the image so that it contains the correct amount of information.*

More isn't better; it's simply more. Next time you prepare to scan for print, use this information to put your scanner on a diet. There is, of course, another alternative—if you're one of the brave experimenters who's using a stochastic or frequency-modulated type of screening for print output, you can forget about halftoning entirely, which may save you even more megabytes.

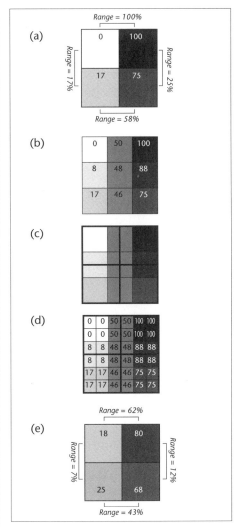

Figure 7–8   *courtesy ImageXPress, Inc.*

Including excess pixels in an image can result in a loss of contrast and detail after halftoning. (a) Adjacent pixel values in an image that has a 1.4:1 ppi-to-lpi ratio. (b) Adjacent pixel values in an image that has a 2:1 ppi-to-lpi ratio. (c) The imagesetter's RIP averages all values within a halftone cell to derive one value per halftone dot. (d) The RIP adds all tone values in each cell and divides them by the number of cell components (here, nine). (e) The result of this averaging process is reduced contrast and detail when compared with the version before halftoning (b) or with an image that contains just the right amount of data (a).

Stochastic and Frequency-Modulated (FM) Screening

Over the past several years, various new digital screening technologies have emerged to rival halftoning. Among the most promising are those referred to as *stochastic* or *frequency-modulated (FM)* screening. Whereas digital halftoning uses regular patterns—variably sized dots spaced at fixed intervals—FM screening technologies use smaller, fixed-size dots placed at irregular locations. This approach eliminates the need for halftone screen frequencies and screen angles, and with it the problem of visible moiré patterns that can appear when halftoned screens of different ink colors align improperly with one another. Without the differences between horizontal scanning angles and halftone screen angles to worry about, a scanned image doesn't need to contain as much information in order to output well at a given printer resolution. That translates to a 33 percent reduction in scanning resolution (and a considerably smaller file size!) if you will be using FM screening rather than digital halftoning for your final output.

Caution: *Don't rush out to look for stochastic screening software or a service provider that uses FM screening technologies just yet. FM screening is a young technology and has a tendency to increase the amount of dot gain incurred during the printing process.*

Resizing and Resampling Images

In an ideal world, you would scan all originals so that they contained exactly the right amount of information for output from the outset, with no further changes in sizing or resolution necessary later. Alas, workflows (especially group workflows) rarely follow such an ideal path. The person doing the scanning may not be in communication with the editor, designer, or production professional who specifies the output dimensions; a project may be undefined at the time scanning occurs; or plans can simply change. Whatever the cause, it's often necessary to adapt the size, resolution, or amount of information in an image as output time nears. In this section of the chapter, we advise you on the best techniques for maintaining image integrity while handling these tasks.

Determining Output Resolution and Maximum Output Size

For many output media, including computer-based presentations, multimedia, film recorders, and video, output size is fixed (see Table 7–1). If you don't have the right amount of information in the image to start with, you usually have only two choices—either jettison pixels through downsampling (no apparent quality loss) or add pixels through interpolation (loss of sharpness and contrast).

The choices are less clear-cut for print publishing professionals. Your first task, before you can decide whether resizing or resampling is necessary, is to determine (a) the appropriate output resolution and (b) the maximum size at which an image can be printed with high quality. If you're using a PostScript-based output device that employs halftone screening technology, the output resolution of the image should be 1.5 times the halftone screen. If you're using a PostScript device with stochastic or FM screening, the output resolution can be as low as 120 dpi at final output size. And if the final output device is a continuous-tone printer, output resolution can range from 75 to 100 percent of the printer resolution.

Once you have the optimum output resolution figured out, you can easily calculate the maximum output size. Simply divide the number of pixels in each dimension of the image by the output resolution (Table 7–1 shows another way to derive this information). So, for example, an image measuring 1,800 pixels wide by 2,250 pixels high and requiring an output resolution of 225 ppi can be printed at a maximum size of 8 × 10 inches. If it needs to be printed at a smaller size, then the image must be downsampled to remove superfluous pixels. If, on the other hand, the final output size must be larger than 8 × 10 inches, you have two choices:

- Decrease the output resolution and leave the amount of information in the image unchanged. If the decrease in resolution is minor, the visible effect on image quality will be negligible. But if the resolution dips substantially below what's necessary to maintain the 1.5 resolution-to-screen-frequency ratio, the lack of enough information to produce halftone dots accurately could compromise the tonal integrity and detail in the image.

- Add pixels to the image through resampling. The interpolation process—which doesn't add "real" detail—compromises the sharpness and crisp detail of the image, a defect for which you can partially compensate with the help of an unsharp masking filter. (Be careful with unsharp masking on low-resolution images—anything but a light application might create unwanted halo effects.)

Changing Output Size or Resolution Only

Perhaps you're in luck—the image that you're preparing for output does contain just the right amount of information, but you need to change the output resolution or dimensions. As long as you lock the file size when altering dimensions or resolution (see Figure 7–9), this type of resizing involves no quality loss, since *there is a reciprocal relationship between resolution and output dimensions.* Increasing resolution automatically reduces the print dimensions of an image, and decreasing resolution automatically increases the print dimensions (Figure 7–10).

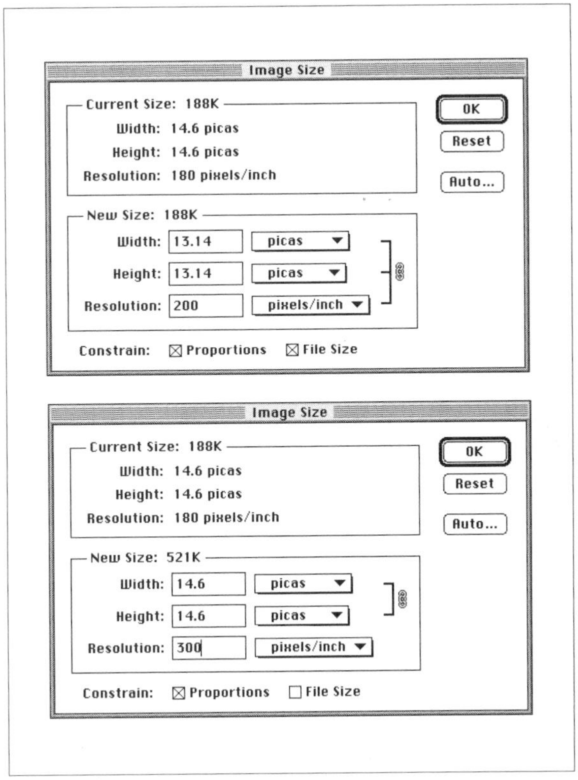

Figure 7–9

*Most major image-editing packages (here, Adobe Photoshop) allow you to choose whether to constrain the file size when changing resolution or dimensions. Constraining the file size (**top**) keeps the amount of information in the image fixed and permits changes to resolution and output dimensions only. Changing resolution or dimensions with the file size unconstrained (**bottom**) resamples the image, adding or subtracting pixels with the consequent risk of degradation.*

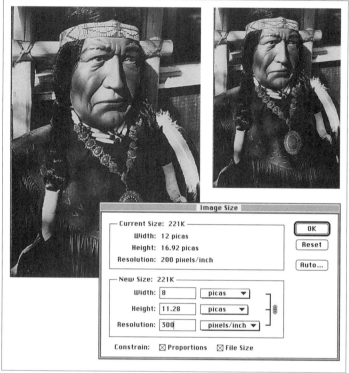

Figure 7–10

© Emil Ihrig

When file size is constrained, increasing resolution (here, from 200 ppi to 300 ppi) automatically reduces image output size, and decreasing resolution automatically increases output size.

Resampling Images

Many graphics professionals experience confusion over the difference between resizing and resampling. Resizing involves changing resolution or output dimensions while keeping the amount of information constant. *Resampling*, on the other hand, always involves a change to the amount of information in an image and can involve changes to resolution, dimensions, or both. Since it entails interpolation and averaging, resampling is a solution that you should use only when the original scan contains either too much or too little information for high-quality output.

Graphic arts professionals use the term *downsampling* to refer to a reduction of the number of pixels in an image and *upsampling* or *interpolation* to describe an increase in the number of pixels. Pixel-value averaging occurs in both cases. Correct downsampling eliminates unusable detail, while upsampling adds pseudodetail. Both involve compromises to image quality, but whereas downsampling rarely results in visible degradation because it usually accompanies a reduction in size, upsampling almost always does.

There are basically two ways to resample an image—through freehand scaling or through an Image Size–type dialog box where you specify changes to resolution or dimensions numerically. The second method is much more precise and gives you exact control over how much information to add or subtract.

Resampling Guidelines

- Use the highest-quality resampling algorithm available to your image-editing package to minimize visible loss. Photoshop, for example, offers a choice of three options: Bicubic, Bilinear, and Nearest Neighbor. The Bicubic option offers the most sophisticated pixel-value averaging; the Bilinear method produces a softer look that lessens the likelihood of artifacts; and Nearest Neighbor is fast but results in more visible jaggedness (see Figure C–14 in the color gallery).

- Avoid resampling the same image more than once. A loss occurs every time you change the amount of information in an image, so it's important to avoid courting second-, third- and fourth-generation degradation.

If You Want to Determine . . .	And You Know . . .	Use This Formula:
Aspect ratio, computer-based media or video	Monitor resolution Video resolution	Width ÷ Height
Enlargement factor	Original dimensions Desired output dimensions	Output dimensions ÷ Original dimensions
File size in bytes, bitmap or line art mode	Scanning resolution Dimensions of original	[Horizontal dimensions × Vertical dimensions × (Scanning resolution)^2] ÷ 8
File size in bytes, grayscale mode	Scanning resolution Dimensions of original	Horizontal dimensions × Vertical dimensions × (Scanning resolution)^2
File size in bytes, RGB mode	Scanning resolution Dimensions of original	[Horizontal dimensions × Vertical dimensions × (Scanning resolution)^2] × 3
File size in bytes, CMYK mode	Scanning resolution Dimensions of original	[Horizontal dimensions × Vertical dimensions × (Scanning resolution)^2] × 4
Maximum number of tones per color, halftoning device output	Printer resolution Screen frequency	(Printer resolution ÷ Screen frequency)^2 + 1
Maximum output dimensions, halftoning device output (conventional screening technologies)	Number of pixels along each dimension Screen frequency	Number of pixels ÷ (Screen frequency × 1.5)
Maximum output dimensions, halftoning device output (stochastic screening technologies)	Number of pixels along largest dimension Screen frequency	Number of pixels ÷ Screen frequency
Maximum output dimensions, continuous-tone printer output	Number of pixels, largest dimension /Printer resolution	(Number of pixels ÷ Printer resolution) ÷ 0.75 or 1.0
Output resolution, halftoning device output (conventional screening technologies)	Screen frequency	Screen frequency × 1.5
Scanning resolution, halftoning device output (conventional screening technologies)	Original and output dimensions Screen frequency Optical resolution of input device	Enlargement factor × 1.5 × Screen frequency (or next highest integral scanning resolution)
Scanning resolution, halftoning device output (stochastic screening technologies)	Dimensions of original Output dimensions	Enlargement factor × 1.2
Scanning resolution, continuous-tone device output	Dimensions of original Output dimensions Printer resolution	Enlargement factor × Printer resolution OR Enlargement factor × Printer resolution × 0.75
Scanning resolution, line art	Dimensions of original Output dimensions Printer resolution	Enlargement factor × Printer resolution (up to 1,200 dpi), using the next highest integral scanning resolution
Scanning resolution, film recorder output	Dimensions of original Format of original Output dimensions in pixels (determined by format of film recorder media format)	Width of broadest dimension of output media, in pixels ÷ Width or height of original (depending on vertical or horizontal format)
Scanning resolution, computer-based media output	Dimensions of original Monitor resolution, aspect ratio	Vertical monitor resolution (in pixels) ÷ Narrowest dimension of original
Scanning resolution, video output	Dimensions of original Video resolution	Vertical dimension of video frame, in pixels ÷ Narrowest dimension of original

Table 7–1

Calculating Aspect Ratio, Enlargement Factor, File Size, Output Resolution, Scanning Resolution, and Output Tonal Range

■ Downsampling is safer than upsampling in terms of minimizing the loss to image quality, especially if the output size of the image is reduced in the process. The detail lost in downsampling is actually detail that couldn't be printed anyway.

Mastering resolution is one of the most important aspects of scanning, but it's hardly the whole story. In Chapter 8, we'll review common scanning procedures step by step for a hands-on look at how to obtain the highest-quality scanned images.

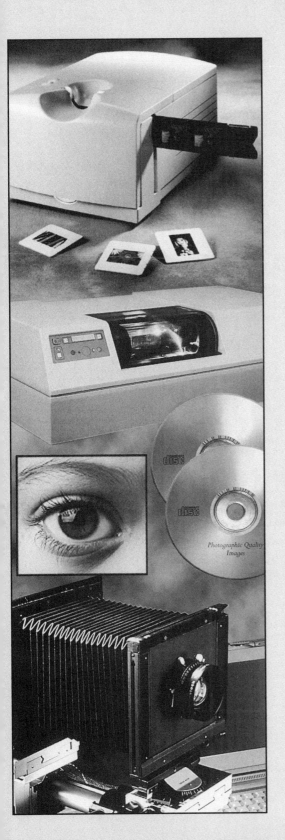

8

Hands-On Scanning

Scanning software options are growing more sophisticated by the day. No longer is it necessary to obtain a "raw" scan and then handle all the "important" manipulation tasks in an image-editing package. Today, midrange flatbed and transparency scanner plug-ins routinely allow you to adjust tonality, balance color, and sharpen images on the fly, before a single pixel ever finds its way onto your hard drive. Higher-end options such as removal of previous halftone screening, batch scanning, and automatic generation of color separations are trickling down from drum scanners (which have long boasted such capabilities) to more modest desktop scanners.

Our basic assumption in this chapter is that it's to your advantage to perform as many image-processing tasks as possible *before* scanning. *Preprocessing* allows you to capture exactly the data you need, which results in a higher-quality image, saves time during the production process, and allows you to focus your attention on more creative image-manipulation tasks such as retouching, selective enhancement, and montaging. *Post-processing* (what you do in Photoshop or another image-editing package after scanning) results in loss of both image data and time.

111

Of course, you need to know as much as possible about the output specifications for an image in order to make preprocessing work. Now you know why we've been harping on this theme all the way through the book!

> **❝** *It's to your advantage to perform as many image-processing tasks as possible before scanning.* **❞**

Getting a Good Scan: An Overview

Think of this chapter as the equivalent of a "Quick Start" guide in a software manual. We'll take you through a tour of the essential and optional steps involved in getting a good scan. The order of steps you follow with your own scanner may vary, depending on the level of sophistication of the accompanying software; just skip the steps that don't apply to you.

Here, in a nutshell, are the basic procedures for obtaining a quality scan:

1. Physically prepare the scanner for use.
2. Prepare and position the original(s) in the scanner.
3. Activate the scanner plug-in or software.
4. Check the scanner's preference settings.
5. Choose the correct type of original.
6. Select a scanning mode.
7. Select a destination depending on whether you plan to view and edit the image on the monitor or output it directly to a printing device.
8. Prescan the original.
9. Crop and otherwise adjust the preview.
10. Set resolution and sizing.
11. Adjust highlight and shadow points, gamma, and related tonal settings.
12. Correct for color cast or other color imbalances.
13. If you're using a drum scanner, sharpen the prescan.
14. Scan the image.

For our examples in this chapter, we'll be using the UMAX PowerLook and its accompanying MagicScan software. If your scanner doesn't offer all the preprocessing tools we describe here, you'll need to handle the missing steps through post-processing in an image-editing package. But whether you process an image before or after scanning, the principles and important steps are the same. Bon voyage, and happy scanning!

Preparing the Scanner

The location of a scanner is important. If you're using a desktop scanner (flatbed, transparency, or baby drum), position it absolutely level on a stable surface to avoid vibration, which can induce scanning artifacts and even damage scanner components. Avoid banging scanner lids for the same reason.

Other environmental factors are important, too. Keep the area around the scanner as dust-free as possible so that those ugly speckles we documented in Chapter 6 don't find their way onto your originals. Electrical interference is another culprit that can damage the scanner and generate weird scanning errors. To avoid it, move the scanner away from fluorescent light sources or halogen lamps that use a step-down transformer. Use a shielded ferrite cable (some manufacturers supply them) to connect the scanner to your computer or SCSI devices, and invest in line-conditioning equipment.

If you're working with a flatbed or transparency scanner, allow it to warm up for at least 30 minutes before use. The light sources in such scanners brighten and change color temperature after the equipment has been turned on for awhile, resulting in better exposures and scans with a broader tonal range.

Finally, make sure the scanner has been calibrated recently (if it's not auto-calibrating). If you use a CMS (see Chapter 5) or if the scanner includes its own color management setup, ensure that the profile for your scanner isn't more than a month or two old.

Positioning the Artwork

Placing originals properly in the scanner eliminates the time-consuming necessity of rotating a previously digitized image by software and can help you avoid damage to sensitive artwork. For flatbed scanners that digitize reflective artwork only, correct positioning means placing the original face down, dead center on the plate. (The fluorescent lamps used in most flatbed scanners are susceptible to *fall-off*, a phenomenon that produces better illumination near the center and less at the outer edges of an original.) If you'll be scanning a slide or transparency on a flatbed that has a transparency adapter, place the original face down *and* upside down. Some scanners with transparency adapters require you to place guides on the flatbed plate to block out extraneous light. Take care that the original is absolutely straight; even a degree or two of rotation makes an image look annoyingly lopsided once it's been digitized. Post-scanning rotation always incurs some data loss.

In film and transparency scanners, the location of the lens and CCD array determine the correct orientation of originals. (A typical placement is upside down and backward.) Some dedicated 35mm slide scanners allow you simply to drop the original into a slot. Mixed-media scanners provide separate types of holders for slides, film negatives, and larger-format transparencies.

Preparing originals for drum scanners takes more time and work than for other types of scanners. Since nothing separates a drum from the light source other than a few millimeters of air, artwork must be securely mounted so that it doesn't fall off and suffer damage as the drum revolves at high speeds. The traditional means of affixing transmissive originals to a drum was with a special scanner solution—first dipping the original in the solution, then wrapping it evenly and smoothly on the drum surface, and finally covering the original with transparent acetate. That's a delicate process that doesn't work with reflective originals. These days, the use of tape is becoming more common, as is the use of *anti-Newton spray* to prevent the ring-like scanning artifacts that are caused by air pockets between the mounted original and the drum surface. The advent of removable drums makes it possible for drum scanner operators to mount one set of originals on a second drum while the first is spinning, which saves time.

Activating Scanner Software

Once everything is physically in place, it's time to activate the scanner software, which is typically either a Photoshop-compatible plug-in or a stand-alone software package. In Photoshop and image-editing programs that have a similar architecture, accessing the plug-in is a matter of choosing the appropriate command from the File:Acquire submenu. High-end drum and flatbed scanners provide comprehensive scanning and image-editing packages that do away with the need for a separate program.

Tip: *If you use a popular brand of flatbed or transparency scanner with an image-editing package that supports Photoshop-compatible plug-ins, you may be able to use ScanPrepPro from ImageXpress to automatically adjust your scanner's settings in the background. Activate ScanPrep and define the scanner model, type of original, tonal key, condition, input dimensions, desired resolution-to-screen-frequency ratio (see Chapter 7), output type, press conditions, and paper stock. Then activate your scanner plug-in. ScanPrepPro will already have set up the scanner interface to process the image automatically for optimum output conditions.*

After you access the scanner software, there are a few steps you should take *before* obtaining a prescan so that the preview is accurate: adjust the scanner's preferences, assign the type of original, and select a scanning mode.

Setting Scanner Preferences

It's easy to overlook a scanner's preference settings, but they can save you time for repetitive input tasks and

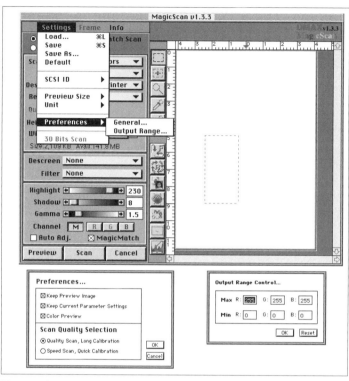

Figure 8–1
Scanner preferences for UMAX MagicScan (PowerLook) affect default scanner settings, calibration speed, and tonal range.

assure you of better image quality. Scanner preferences vary from one model to another; Figure 8–1 shows the preference options for the UMAX PowerLook flatbed scanner.

Selecting the Type of Original

If you're using a flatbed scanner with transparency attachment, a multimedia transparency scanner, or a drum scanner, you need to communicate what type of original you're about to digitize. Choices usually include reflective, transparent, or negative, or may define the transparency format for transparency scanners. Don't overlook this setting; depending on the scanner, it could impact the brightness of the light source, the focus of the lens, and the available imaging area.

Selecting a Scanning Mode

The scanning mode refers to the bit depth or color depth used in digitizing an image (see Chapter 5). Typical scanning modes are bitmap or line art (1-bit black and white), grayscale (8-bit), and RGB color (24 or more bits). Some scanners also let you scan in 8-bit color, which can be useful for images that will be used in multimedia and presentations. If you scan in grayscale, investigate whether your scanner simply derives grayscale information from all three RGB channels or from a single channel. Some scanners let you choose which method to use and even let you pick the channel on which to base the grayscale image. Figure 8–2 shows the scanning mode and grayscale scanning options offered by the UMAX PowerLook.

Tip: *The green channel in an RGB image contains the broadest tonal range and is the best channel on which to base a grayscale scan if your main concern is with detail. If an original is dark, base the grayscale scan on the red channel, which tends to record the brightest values. If an original is too light, base the grayscale scan on the blue channel, which generally records the darkest values.*

Drum scanners usually offer a CMYK scanning option as well. This actually involves scanning the original in RGB mode and then immediately converting the image to CMYK through the scanner's firmware. See Chapter 5 for a discussion of when scanning in CMYK is advisable. If you do opt for CMYK scanning, however, you should first input the desired color prepress options in the scanner software to ensure that total ink limits, black generation amount, UCR, GCR, UCA, and other settings related to press conditions are correct. Otherwise, the colors in the final printed image may not turn out as you expect. (See *Preparing Digital Images for Print*, also in the Osborne/McGraw-Hill Digital Pro series, for more about color prepress options.)

Selecting a Destination

Some scanner software packages ask you to define the *destination* of the scanned image. This setting has to do with what happens next in the production workflow and affects how the scanner renders colors. If you plan to edit the image on screen, choose Display or Monitor display as the destination. If you'll simply be placing the un-retouched scan in a layout for PostScript output, select a halftone printer option. Some scanners include a continuous-tone printer option for use when the final output device is a dye sublimation or high-end inkjet printer rather than an imagesetter. Figure 8–2 shows destination options for the UMAX PowerLook.

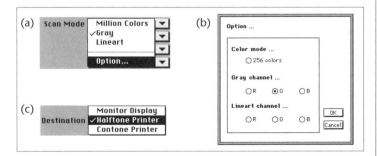

Figure 8–2

Options for scanning mode (a), color, grayscale, and line art channel (b), and destination (c) for the UMAX PowerLook

Caution: *If your scanner has a Destination setting and you'll be using an image for several types of output, you'll need to generate a separate scan for each type to ensure that colors render properly for each output device.*

Note: *In some scanner software interfaces, selecting a Halftone option tells the scanner to pre-halftone the image at a given screen frequency, digitizing the image as black and white halftone dots rather than as color or grayscale. If your final output device will be a PostScript printer or imagesetter, don't pre-halftone an image unless you want to use extremely low halftone screen frequencies and unusual dot patterns for special effects.*

Prescanning the Original

At this point, you're ready to prescan the original. A *prescan* is a low-resolution preview of the original that helps you determine an approximate crop and the best tonal and color settings for the scan. Be sure to select the correct kind of preview (grayscale or color) before prescanning. Scanners vary widely in the quality and maneuverability of their preview images. You'll have an easier time defining accurate input settings (and getting a good base scan) if your scanner offers large or variable-size preview windows, easy-to-use cropping tools, multiple levels of zooming, and real-time changes to the preview as you alter tonal or color settings. Drum and flatbed scanners of the caliber used in color prepress houses and service bureaus often feature full-screen previews that facilitate viewing highly accurate detail.

Cropping and Sizing the Preview

Crop the preview image so that only the part of the original you want to use gets digitized. Most scanners offer at least a rudimentary marquee that you can resize with the mouse to define the crop area; many allow you to set the crop area numerically. Cropping is more accurate if a scanner lets you change preview window size or zoom in on the preview one or more times to see detail. Most scanner interfaces show you the input dimensions of the cropped area as you adjust the marquee.

Adjusting Size and Setting Resolution

Defining the appropriate scanning resolution is one of the most important input tasks. If you scan in too little information, the image will look jagged and pixelized after final output. If you scan in too much (the more common case), you're wasting hard disk space, processing power, and output dollars and may also compromise image quality (see Chapter 7).

Scanner software may determine input resolution automatically, or you may have to do it yourself. If you need to calculate your own, see Chapter 7 for guidelines. Automated calculation usually takes one of the following forms:

- You enter an enlargement factor, an output screen frequency, and a halftoning or quality factor, and the software determines resolution based on these entries plus the cropped dimensions. *Halftoning factor or quality factor should be 1.5, not 2* (see Chapter 7).

- You enter the desired output dimensions, and the software calculates resolution based on this, the quality factor, the line screen, and the cropped dimensions.

Caution: *Few scanner manufacturers recognize the principle of using integral scanner resolutions to preserve image quality, so you may need to override the calculated resolution manually.*

Tonal Adjustment

You can alter the way a scanner reproduces the content of an original by adjusting tonality, color, or both. Always adjust tonality first to ensure a proper range of tones from light to dark, good detail in the midtones, and eye-pleasing brightness and contrast relationships throughout the image. Once you've established these, eliminating color casts and enhancing color makes better sense.

Tonal adjustment is important for any image, but it's essential for scans that will be output to print. The interaction between printing press type, paper stock absorbency, and printing ink characteristics requires that the tones in scanned images be compressed to less than a full range (0 to 100 percent) for output; otherwise, detail in the lightest areas of the image will drop out and detail in the darkest areas will turn to mud. Press, paper, and ink are also responsible for the phenomenon of *dot gain*, whereby midtone values in an image darken when printed. One of the tasks of tonal adjustment is to precompensate for dot gain by remapping midtone values.

Tip: *Anticipated dot gain and recommended tonal range limits depend on the particular paper stock and ink standards used for a print job. Always check with your print vendor to obtain these specifications before scanning. If you can't get this information at the time scanning takes place, scan with a full range of tones and don't apply any tonal adjustments*

to the prescan. Instead, handle tonal adjustment as a post-processing step in an image-editing program.

For best results, apply prescanning tonal adjustments in a specific order. Adjust the white and black points first, then the gamma, and finally the other tonal ranges in the image, if necessary. The sections that follow describe how to make these adjustments and their respective roles in image reproduction.

Tools for Tonal Adjustment

Scanner interfaces offer a variety of tools and techniques for tweaking tonality. Common options include numerical entry, slider controls, histograms, picker tools, editable tonal curves, and automatic tonal adjustments. Here's a brief description of how each technique works (refer to Figure 8–3 for visual examples):

- **Numerical entry**—This type of control lets you assign minimum and maximum brightness levels for a grayscale or color image using values from 0 to 255 (see "Setting Highlight and Shadow Points," following). A value of 0 corresponds to black, while a value of 255 corresponds to white. Changing these values limits the tonal range of the scan without altering relative brightness and contrast relationships within the image.

- **Highlight, Shadow, and Gamma sliders**—Many scanner interfaces include a simple slider and text box that you can use to remap highlight, shadow, and midtone values. Gamma values below the default 1.0 darken the midtones, while gamma values above 1.0 lighten them.

Tip: *An average key image typically requires a gamma setting of 1.5 to 1.6. Use a gamma of 1.8 to 1.9 for low-key and underexposed originals. High-key images should be scanned using a gamma of 1.2 to 1.3 (see Chapter 6).*

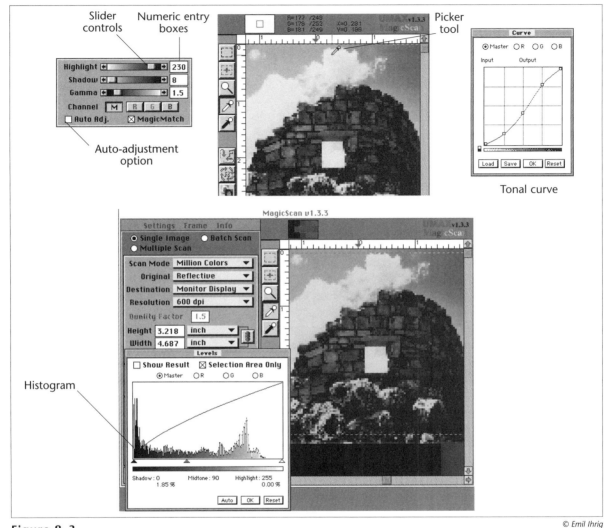

Figure 8–3

© Emil Ihrig

The types of tonal adjustment tools found in the UMAX MagicScan interface are typical of those found in many scanner plug-ins and software packages.

- **Histograms**—These graphs show the distribution of tonal values in the original artwork (see Chapter 6). If the histogram provided by your scanner's software is editable, you can use numbers or sliders to remap highlight, shadow, and midtone values.

- **Picker tools**—Some scanning interfaces include eyedropper-like tools that you can use to select highlight and shadow values interactively from the prescan. Selecting a pixel with a highlight picker tool automatically sets that pixel's value as the brightest tone and remaps it to white. Clicking on a pixel with a shadow picker tool determines the darkest tone and remaps it to black. Some scanner software packages also include a picker tool for setting the midtone value, which effectively adjusts the gamma.

- **Editable tone curves**—Tone curves are arguably the most flexible and sophisticated type of tonal adjustment tool. They allow you to remap brightness and contrast levels at any number of tonal points, not just at the extremes and midtones as with other types of tools. Most scanner interfaces that feature tonal curves also allow you to load and save curve settings for use with similar images.

- **Auto-adjustment options**—Most scanning software offers an "Auto-adjust" or "Auto-exposure" option that redistributes tones in the original to include the full range from white to black. Selecting this option alters contrast relationships throughout the image. The quality of auto-exposure options varies widely among scanners and may not give you the precise control over tonal adjustment that you get with curves, picker tools, or histograms. It's useful for images that will be output to computer-based media, but not for images that will be printed (see "Setting Highlight and Shadow Points," following).

Setting Highlight and Shadow Points

The *highlight point* and *shadow point* of a digital image (sometimes called *white point* and *black point*) are the brightest and darkest tonal values in an image that still contain detail. The type of output planned for an image determines how you should set these points. Images destined for any medium other than print should contain a full range of tones from black to white; in such cases, set the highlight to zero (or 0 percent) and the shadow point to 255 (or 100 percent), or use an Auto-adjust option to force tonal distribution across the entire spectrum.

That's not the case for print media, however. When an image will be output to print, it's common practice to remap the original's white and black points during scanning—setting the brightest value in the image to darker than white, and the darkest value to lighter than black. This process compresses the tonal range for printing purposes so that light details don't drop out to white and details in the darkest areas of the image don't become an undifferentiated black. See Figure C–15 in the color gallery.

Note: Technically, white point and black point define the values that should print as pure white and solid black, respectively. But as the electronic publishing industry has evolved, common usage has made these terms interchangeable with highlight and shadow point.

Some originals contain *specular highlights*—content that *should* appear pure white (without detail) in print. If your scanner's software includes a highlight picker tool, you can retain these extremely bright areas as white in the scan by choosing as a highlight a pixel that is slightly darker than the specular highlights. This light (but not white) value then becomes the lightest level of detail when the image is scanned, and areas in the original that are even lighter remain white. You can achieve the same goal with an editable histogram by dragging input sliders to the tonal extremes, or with a tonal curve by steepening the angle at the highlight end of the diagonal.

Together, press type and paper stock determine the correct highlight and shadow points to assign to images for a particular print job. Table 8–1 lists typical recommended highlight and shadow points based on press conditions. These are general parameters that may vary from one paper stock or press type to the next, so consult your print vendor before assigning specific values. If you're scanning a color original, it's generally best to adjust highlight and shadow points for the master channel first, and then make additional adjustments to individual color channels if necessary. Figure 8–4

Press Type/ Paper Stock	Recommended Highlight Point	Recommended Shadow Point	Typical Dot Gain
Sheet Fed/Coated	1 to 4%	93 to 98%	4%
Sheet Fed/Uncoated	3 to 5%	90 to 95%	8%
Heat Set/Coated	3 to 5%	85 to 95%	14–20%
Heat Set/Uncoated	3 to 7%	80 to 93%	18–25%
Newspaper/Coated	3 to 5%	78 to 90%	20–26%
Newspaper/Uncoated	3 to 5%	75 to 85%	22–28%
Newspaper/Newsprint	2 to 7%	72 to 85%	26–30%

Table 8–1

selected data courtesy ImageXpress, Inc.

Typical White Point, Black Point, and Dot Gain Settings for Standard Press and Paper Combinations

shows how various adjustments to the highlight and shadow points affect tonal compression and contrast in a scanned image.

Tip: *Let the tonal character of an original guide you in setting black and white points (see Chapter 6). When an original contains large areas of shadow detail that you want to reproduce, reduce the shadow value by a few percentage points below what's recommended for your press conditions. Conversely, if an original contains large areas of highlight detail, increase the highlight value by a few percentage points above the recommended level.*

As you can see from Figure 8–4, remapping the highlight and shadow points alone, without making other tonal adjustments, tends to

Highlight 0%, Shadow 100%   Highlight 3%, Shadow 95%   Highlight 7%, Shadow 90%   Highlight 10%, Shadow 75%

Figure 8–4

© Emil Ihrig

Remapping the highlight and shadow values of an original, without altering the gamma, causes the scanner to compress tonal range and flatten contrast.

flatten image contrast. To reintroduce eye-pleasing contrast after setting the white and black points, you next need to adjust the midtones, also known as *correcting the gamma*.

Adjusting the Gamma

Whenever you alter the midtone values of an image, you automatically affect other tonal and contrast relationships in the image as well, often dramatically. This basic fact has to do with the nonlinear way in which the human eye perceives brightness. If you lighten the midtones, you also lighten darker and brighter areas of an image; if you darken the midtones, darker and brighter areas get darkened, too (Figure 8–5). So when you correct the gamma of an original for scanning purposes, you're actually manipulating brightness and contrast relationships throughout the image.

Gamma correction has several uses:

- It can help compensate for exposure problems in an original—drawing out detail lurking in an underexposed or overexposed photo, for example.

- It can intensify contrast and detail in a low-key or high-key image. (See Figure C–16 in the color gallery.)

- It's a great way to reintroduce contrast into any image that has been flattened by white and black point adjustments.

- It's an effective technique for compensating for dot gain that occurs during the printing process.

Most scanner software packages offer multiple techniques for adjusting the midtones. Options may include a numerical gamma setting, a Gamma slider in a histogram, a curve for

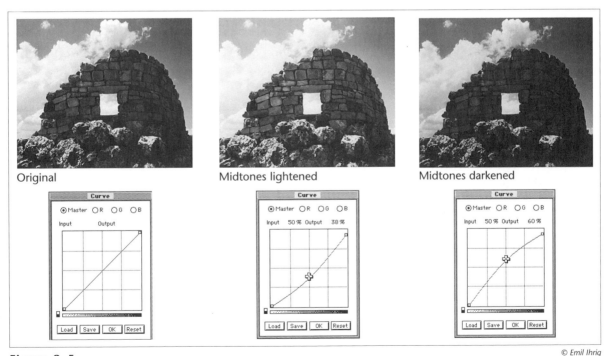

Original   Midtones lightened   Midtones darkened

© Emil Ihrig

Figure 8–5

Adjusting midtone values prior to scanning alters brightness and contrast relationships throughout an image.

manipulating midtones as well as other tonal values, or all of the above. When using a numerical setting, increase the gamma above 1.0 to brighten the midtones and reduce it below 1.0 to darken them. If your scanner interface lets you adjust tonality using sliders, move the Gamma or midtone slider to the right to lighten midtones or to the left to darken them. If tonal curves are your preferred modus operandi, you can lighten midtones by generating an upward-bulging, convex curve and darken them by creating a downward-bulging, concave curve.

Gamma Correction and Dot Gain

Gamma or midtone correction to a prescan is especially useful in compensating for dot gain. *Dot gain* refers to the tendency of halftone dots to spread and darken based on the interaction between press, paper stock (or film), and ink. The figure that print vendors usually quote describes the amount of gain at the 50 percent halftone dot, where dot gain is heaviest. The amount of gain tapers off toward the tonal extremes, though it's heavier in the shadows than in the highlights.

There's a great deal of confusion in the industry over whether dot gain is a relative measurement or an absolute measurement. This issue is critical because it determines how you should *compensate* for dot gain. So which is it? It all depends on who's quoting the figures. Print industry professionals who learned their trade before the advent of desktop publishing quote dot gain *relative* to the 50 percent (mid-tone) dot. To these individuals, a 20 percent dot gain means that the tonal value at the 50 percent dot darkens by 20 percent *of* 50 percent, or 10 percent in absolute terms—a 50 percent gray therefore becomes 60 percent when printed. To professionals weaned on the desktop, on the other hand, dot gain is measured in absolute terms—20 percent dot gain means that the 50 percent dot prints as 70 percent

gray. Whenever a print representative quotes a dot gain percentage to you, find out whether the quoted terms are relative or absolute; it could make the difference between a perfect tonal balance or one that's too dark or too light.

With this information in mind, it's possible to correct gamma to precompensate for dot gain. Let's say you're scanning an average-key image and anticipate a 20 percent dot gain measured in absolute terms. If your scanner interface offers tonal curves (our preferred technique), drag the 50 percent point down to a little above 30 percent (remember, the amount of dot gain is heavier at the midtones than in the lighter portion of the tonal range). The scanned image will look lighter than the original in the mid-tones, but when it's printed, the 30+ percent dot will darken to 50 percent—just where it should be. If you anticipate a 20 percent dot gain measured in *relative* terms, drag the 50 percent point on the curve down to 40 percent (20 percent of 50 percent = 10 percent *less* than 50 percent). Let the tonal character of the original guide you—don't blindly compensate for the midtones alone if a substantial portion of the subject matter appears in the shadows, for example.

When adjusting color images, always apply gamma correction to the composite image first. Then, if necessary, tweak the midtones in individual RGB or CMYK channels separately.

Tip: When requesting dot gain specifications for a print job, ask for the total amount of dot gain from film to press rather than from proof to press. Many print vendors quote the latter figure, which is lower and not as accurate for an all-digital production process.

Adjusting Quartertones

Remapping the highlight, shadow, and mid-tone values of an original prior to scanning sometimes isn't effective enough to achieve the results you want for print output. To give an image real "punch," it's often necessary to adjust tonality at four or five points, not just three. The two additional points are the *quartertones* that correspond to the 25 and 75 percent values on a tonal curve. Let the tonal character of an original guide you in determining how to shape a prescan curve. Refer to Figure C–16 in the color gallery for examples and follow these general guidelines to add contrast and intensify detail:

- **High-key images**—Darken the three-quarter tones (the 75 percent tones) and the midtones slightly, but leave the quarter tones (the 25 percent value) unchanged.

- **Low-key images**—Lighten the three-quarter tones significantly and brighten the midtones and quarter tones to a lesser extent.

- **Average images**—Create an S-shaped curve in which the midtone remains fixed at 50 percent, the three-quarter tones are darkened slightly, and the quartertones are brightened.

Enhancing and Correcting Color

Preprocessing color enhancement and correction tools vary widely among scanners, with the most sophisticated options—masking and automatic color separation, for example—found chiefly in the software packages that accompany desktop and high-end drum scanners. However, even most midrange and low-end scanners provide tools that can eliminate color casts and adjust hue and saturation in the prescan. In some cases, the same tools that help you adjust tone can assist you in adjusting color relationships. Some scanner interfaces provide specialized tools for these purposes.

Never attempt color correction on a prescan unless your system has been calibrated, either manually or through color management software (see Chapter 5).

Caution: Make all necessary tonal adjustments to the prescan before *you attempt color correction. If you set highlight, shadow, midtone, and quarter tone values after performing color enhancement, colors in the image will shift, perhaps dramatically.*

Correcting Color Casts

Photographic prints, slides, and transparencies often display a noticeable color cast due to the color characteristics of the film, processing errors, or the lighting conditions under which an image was captured (see Chapter 6). Colors in night shots taken under fluorescent lighting, for example, often shift toward green.

Some scanner software can automatically detect color casts and remove them at the click of a button. If your scanner doesn't offer this option, you can still eliminate color casts prior to scanning by reducing the amount of the unwanted color in the prescan and shifting it toward the complementary color. Intuitive methods for achieving this goal include

- Using tonal curves or histograms to adjust color on a channel-by-channel basis

- Adjusting hue and saturation

- Balancing color

We'll examine basic techniques for eliminating color casts using each of these methods.

Detecting Color Casts in the Prescan

Not all color casts are visible to the naked eye. If your scanner software includes an Eyedropper tool or other type of onscreen densitometer, the easiest way to detect a color cast is to check the prescan RGB color values of an area that should be white or neutral gray. If all three RGB values are identical or extremely close, you're home free. But if they diverge significantly, a color cast is definitely present. The color or colors with the highest value(s) in such cases show the direction of the color shift and indicate which color(s) you must tone down in order to bring the colors back into balance.

Tip: *If an original doesn't contain any neutral colors, prescan it together with a portion of an 18% gray card. These cards, available from photographic supply stores, have a reflective surface value of 50 percent gray and can provide a standardized reference color for prescan correction purposes.*

Working with Channels

Tonal curves and histograms in scanner interfaces usually allow you to adjust color on a channel-by-channel basis and also in the composite image. One way to remove color casts is to adjust the color in the "offending" channel using the same principles as when you adjust tonality in the composite image. The tonal range in which the color cast is most evident should guide you when you're working with curves. If the prescan looks too green in the midtones, for example, a good strategy would be to select the curve for the green channel and reduce the 50 percent value, creating a concave curve that effectively shifts the midtones (and the quarter and three-quarter tones to a lesser extent) away from green and toward

magenta. You can achieve similar effects by reducing the gamma value of the affected channel or moving the midtone slider in a histogram of the affected channel to the left. Figure C–17 in the color gallery shows an example of color cast removal and prescan cast removal options offered by the Polaroid SprintScan35.

Hue and Saturation Adjustments

Another technique for removing color casts is to adjust hue and saturation in the prescan using a color wheel or slider. Figure 8–6 shows how this principle works in the MagicScan plug-in provided with the UMAX PowerLook. In MagicScan's Color Adjustment dialog box, the original prescan appears at the left, while the six-pointed color wheel representing Red, Green, Blue, Cyan, Magenta, and Yellow appears below. Let's say you're working with an original that contains a yellow color cast in the highlights because the photo was taken under incandescent lighting using insufficient flash. Your goal would be to shift the highlight colors away from yellow and toward the complementary color, blue. You could achieve this by first selecting the Highlight option and then clicking in the

Figure 8–6

UMAX MagicScan's Color Adjustment dialog box lets you adjust colors or remove color casts in specific tonal ranges using a color wheel. You can display and choose between two different sample adjustments at a time.

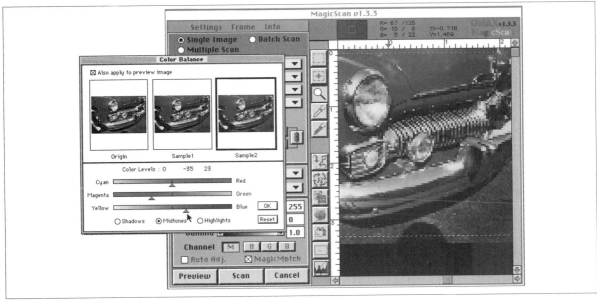

Figure 8–7
UMAX MagicScan's Color Balance dialog box lets you adjust colors or remove color casts in specific tonal ranges by dragging a slider toward the complementary color.

blue area of the color wheel, experimenting with various saturation levels.

Color Balancing Sliders

A third popular prescan technique for eliminating color casts involves the use of color balancing sliders such as the one shown in Figure 8–7. To reduce the excess amount of an unwanted color, simply drag the slider that represents the color toward the opposite end of the slider (the complementary color). Some scanner interfaces allow you to limit the color balancing to specific tonal ranges. Figure C–17 in the color gallery shows an example of color balancing sliders used with the Polaroid SprintScan35.

Other Color Adjustments

Other color adjustments you can make to an original before scanning use tools and techniques similar to those we've already covered.

For example, you might choose to boost color saturation globally or in specific channels for an RGB scan to emphasize certain colors (don't try this willy-nilly with a CMYK scan, or you may exceed the maximum ink coverage allowable for your print project). The content of an original often determines which colors to emphasize. For example, in an photograph of fall foliage in which colors are dull, you might intensify or darken some hues, in effect *introducing* a color cast for content-related purposes (see Figure C–18 in the color gallery). You could use tonal curves, histograms, sliders, or color wheels to increase saturation in the channels that require more dramatic colors.

Creating Color Separations

Our main concern in this book is with obtaining high-quality black and white, grayscale, and RGB color scans that require as little user intervention as possible in later production stages. Although drum scanners and a few high-end flatbed scanners have the ability to create on-the-fly color separations, CMYK scans aren't usually a good idea unless the end user knows all press conditions at the time of scanning and intends simply to drop the scan into a layout without further editing (see the "To Scan or Not to Scan in CMYK" section of Chapter 5). If you obtain a CMYK scan before you have all the necessary information, the ink reduction strategy (GCR or UCR) and the balance between black and the other colors will probably be wrong, with the result that the final image won't print satisfactorily. Most end users find it more convenient to edit color files in the smaller-file RGB mode and convert to CMYK as a post-processing step as the time for final output nears. The next book in this series, *Preparing Digital Images for Print* (Berkeley, CA: Osborne/McGraw-Hill, 1995), explores the process and parameters of creating color separations in much greater detail.

Sharpening and Unsharp Masking

Both the scanning process and the printing process tend to reduce the apparent sharpness of an image. To restore crisp detail, sharpening is therefore almost always necessary, especially for images that will be output to print. Drum scanners typically sharpen an image as scanning takes place. A growing number of desktop scanner plug-ins and software packages offer some type of on-the-fly sharpening option, too, usually either a sharpening filter or an *unsharp masking (USM)* filter. If your scanner doesn't have this capability, you'll need to apply an unsharp masking filter in an image-editing package. The principles are the same whether you sharpen in pre- or post-processing.

Actually, sharpening an image on the fly is advisable only if your scanner can "read ahead"—sampling pixel values and forecasting which pixels need sharpening before the sensing device (CCD or PMT) actually arrives to record the values. Most drum scanners have this capability, but few CCD-based scanners do.

Caution: *High-resolution images that will be printed at very fine line screens (above 150) must be especially sharp to avoid a soft look in print. The perception of detail is the result of significant shifts in the tonal values of adjacent pixels, and as line screen increases, the number of possible tones per halftone dot decreases. Make sure that high-resolution images are razor sharp so that the amount of perceptible detail isn't diminished.*

If both a sharpening and an unsharp masking filter are at your scanner's disposal, choose unsharp masking. All sharpening increases contrast in an image. But whereas sharpening filters simply increase contrast globally, unsharp masking works more subtly, adding contrast only along edges that already contain relatively high contrast between adjacent pixels.

Unsharp masking had its genesis as a by-product of color separation, in the not-so-long-ago days when computers had nothing to do with photography. Prepress camera operators would sharpen a photo by combining positive and negative cyan, magenta, and yellow films to produce an image that appeared sharper overall, emphasizing transitions in high-contrast areas of the two versions while maintaining smooth gradations in lower-contrast areas.

Digital USM filters continue this tradition electronically, applying both blurring and sharpening to produce images that look realistically crisp—as long as you get your settings straight, that is. Too much unsharp masking can create noise or "halo" effects like the example shown in Figure 8–8 and Figure C–19

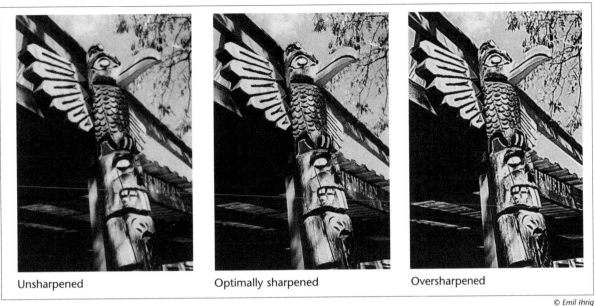

Unsharpened   Optimally sharpened   Oversharpened

© Emil Ihrig

Figure 8–8

*Applying excess amounts of unsharp masking can create an artificial-looking "halo" effect. Compare the leaves, text, and wood grain in the rightmost example with the unsharpened (**left**) and optimally sharpened (**center**) examples.*

in the color gallery. How much is too much? That depends on the content of the image, the output resolution, and the filter settings available in your scanning software.

- **Image content**—Images that contain distant landscapes or cityscapes, long shots of human or animal subjects, and lots of detail can tolerate a fair amount of sharpening. That's not true of images that contain low-detail abstract shapes or close-ups of human or animal faces, where too much detail introduced by excessive sharpening can easily turn ugly.

- **Output resolution**—Noise and halo artifacts from unsharp masking are more likely to appear when the resolution of an image is low. As resolution increases, higher levels of sharpening can be tolerated.

- **Filter settings**—Some unsharp masking filters offer only generic settings, such as "Low,"

"Medium," or "High," which don't give you much control. In such cases, you're probably better off handling unsharp masking as a post-processing step in an image-editing package. You have more control if the filter offered by your scanning software uses adjustable settings which, like those in Adobe Photoshop, let you control the degree (Amount) of sharpening, the distance from each detected edge at which the sharpening takes place (Radius), and the degree of contrast that must be present in order for sharpening to take place (Threshold).

Tip: *The Radius setting is the most critical. Opinions differ, but a good rule of thumb seems to be to set Radius at scanning resolution divided by 200. For example, a Radius setting of 1.0 might achieve optimum sharpening without halos for an image scanned at 200 ppi.*

Tip: *You often can apply a little more sharpening than what seems optimal on your monitor because the halftone screening process tends to soften images slightly.*

Special-Case Scenarios

Some types of originals pose special challenges for scanning. Previously printed visuals and black-and-white drawings are among the most commonly encountered categories of "troublesome" originals. Increasingly, though, scanners at all levels are providing tools for correcting the inherent flaws of these pesky artwork sources.

Descreening Previously Printed Visuals

Artwork that has been previously printed is problematic to scan because it already contains halftone patterning. If you print it again without removing the original halftone screening, moirés will almost certainly be visible in the final because of the interference patterns created by overlapping screens of differing screen angles (Figure 8–9).

Fortunately, more and more scanners allow you to apply a *descreening* filter during the scanning process, which removes previous halftone patterning before it ever has a chance to become part of the digital image. Most such filters accomplish

No descreening applied

 Descreening applied

Figure 8–9

Scanning previously printed images without first removing the old halftone patterning can result in moirés when you halftone and print the image again. Applying a descreening filter on the fly during scanning can remove the existing patterning before it becomes a problem.

this feat by first blurring the image through one or another method (blurring, despeckling, or introduction of random noise) and then sharpening it. The most effective on-the-fly descreening filters let you specify the frequency of the previous screening pattern so that it can be eliminated more accurately.

Tip: *If your scanner has no descreening option, scan at an input resolution that's just a little higher than the screen frequency of the previous halftone patterning (150 ppi for an image printed at 133 lpi, for example). Then, apply a Median or Gaussian Blur type of filter at a low setting and follow up with a moderate application of an unsharp masking filter to restore contrast and detail. Take care with the unsharp masking settings so that the remnants of previous halftone patterning aren't reaccentuated!*

Scanning Line Art

As we mentioned in Chapter 7, black-and-white drawings and logos (and color or grayscale originals that you want to turn into line art) are tough to scan well. It's difficult to align scanner pixels with the edges of fine lines in the original unless there's an even ratio between a line's length or width and the number of pixels that make it up. Scanning at a resolution equal to the resolution of the final output device (up to 1,200 ppi) is one strategy for solving this "jaggy" problem. Following are some others.

- Scan the original at 1:1 size using ScanPrepPro's CopyDot/Fineline option depicted in Figure 8–10. After

scanning the original as a grayscale, CopyDot uses a proprietary combination of processes—interpolation, tonal curve adjustment, unsharp masking, thresholding, and bitmap conversion—to optimize the smooth reproduction of detail present in the original.

- If your scanner offers variable brightness settings, reduce brightness levels until edges begin to fill in with black, forming more solid and continuous lines and shapes.

- If your scanner doesn't support high enough input resolutions, even by interpolation (yes, this is one case where interpolation is acceptable), raise the *threshold* value in the scanner's software—the tonal value at which pixels in the original are assigned as black or white in the scan—until enough pixels turn black to make lines and edges look smooth.

- Scan the black-and-white original as a high-resolution grayscale to preserve some of the subtlety of the original line drawing. As a post-processing step, open the file in an image-editing program and posterize the image to two levels, adjusting the threshold value until lines appear solid.

The Final Scan

If you've followed the steps in this chapter thus far, you've covered all the bases and are ready to scan the original. All high-end scanner software and some desktop scanner

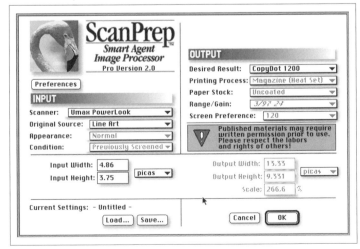

Figure 8–10

ScanPrepPro's CopyDot/Fineline option uses interpolation, tonal curves, and filters in post-processing to optimize the smooth reproduction of fine lines and detail in an original.

packages allow you to load and save entire sets of settings for use with similar originals. If you're uncertain about the correctness of any settings and your scanner supports this type of automation, save the parameters before performing the final scan. Then, if most but not all settings were correct, you can edit the parameters file and make slight alterations without starting the scanning process from scratch.

Post-Processing

Once you've scanned the original and found the results to your liking, you should save the file immediately in a format that matches your project's output requirements (see Chapter 9). What lies ahead are the post-processing steps that include image-processing operations you'll need to apply in an image-editing program if your scanner software didn't supply tools to perform some of the steps we've described in this chapter, or if you need to edit the image in ways not usually supported by desktop scanners. Post-processing steps may include

- Removing dust and scratches with the use of filters or retouching tools

- Creative manipulations such as compositing and layering multiple images, applying filters to create special effects, retouching, and generating original textures

- Sharpening or unsharp masking for print output (recommended for all but PMT-scanned images)

- Tonal adjustment (if not supported by your scanner)

- Color cast removal and color enhancement (if not supported by your scanner)

- Selective enhancement of portions of the image using masks and selection areas

- Adjusting sizing, image resolution, and output resolution prior to final output

- Setting color prepress options and generating final color separations—a task worthy of a book in itself

The preprocessing operations we've outlined in this chapter can be performed by most scanner software, reducing the need for user intervention in routine production tasks later on and freeing up your energies for more creative image-manipulation tasks. What could be more desirable? But if you prefer to handle some of these operations in an image-editing package, or if you'd rather automate your production tasks using a utility such as ScanPrepPro from ImageXpress, you may be interested in the next book in the Osborne/McGraw-Hill Digital Pro series, *Preparing Digital Images for Print*.

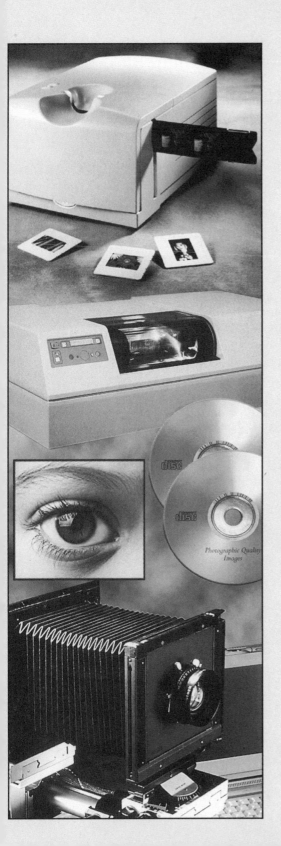

9

File Formats and Compression

File formats are more than a convenience. They determine what kinds of information you can save in a file, how compatible the file will be with various software applications, and how easy it will be to exchange data with others involved in the production process. The choice of how best to save a scanned image depends on several factors—the program you'll be using to post-process the image (if any), the amount of disk storage you have available, whether you'll have to exchange the file with others during the production process, and the eventual output medium. A file often passes through several digital incarnations between the first save and final output, starting off in the native file format of an image-editing package and then being saved in another format for use in a page layout, in a multimedia presentation, or for long-term archival.

Should you save images in a proprietary format native to a particular software application, or in a format that can be read by many different programs? How should you save and name files that may be used by several people working with different software, possibly on multiple platforms? We'll answer these questions and then review the most commonly used file formats for raster

131

images, always with a view to what's going to happen to an image between first scan and final output. See Table 9-1 for a handy reference to file format abbreviations, advantages, and suitability to various output media.

Native Versus Industry-Standard File Formats

Many high-end image-editing and painting applications—Adobe Photoshop, Fractal Design Painter, and HSC Live Picture, for example—allow you to save images in a proprietary file format that's recognized only by that application. Proprietary file formats offer advantages such as smaller file size and the ability to save complex types of information (such as layers, selection masks, vector paths, and channels, in Photoshop's case). If you're working in such an application, it's often a good idea to save the image in the proprietary format, especially if you're going to output the image directly from that application. If you later need to transfer the image to a page layout, to another medium, or to an outside vendor or client, you can resave it at that time to a format that the next user's software can recognize.

Exchanging Files

These days, it's rare that a single person or software package will shepherd an image file all the way from scan to output. Most image data travels through multiple hands, software packages, and platforms before it reaches its final destination. Here are some basic guidelines to keep in mind when saving a file that you'll be passing on to someone else in the workflow.

- Save the file in a standard format that most software applications can read—TIFF or EPS for images intended for print output; PICT or BMP for multimedia or video; and TIFF or PICT for presentations. If a file will definitely be transferred between software applications and several compatible file formats are available, save it in the format that preserves the most comprehensive information about the image data.

- When the file is likely to travel across platforms at least once, use DOS filenaming conventions (a filename of no more than eight characters plus a three-character extension), regardless of which platform the file originated on. Although files saved under Windows 95 can have names up to 255 characters long, it's not safe to assume that PC-platform users of your file have adopted the newer operating system. In addition, every Windows 95 file with a long name also has a truncated alternative filename of the 8.3 DOS variety, which is generated without user control.

- Always use a three-character file extension to assist in easy identification of the file type, even for files that will be used only on Macintosh computers. Table 9–1 lists the accepted file extensions for each file format.

File Formats for Print Media

If a file is intended for eventual placement in a page layout application, you should save it in one of the two standard formats preferred for print output: TIFF or EPS. Avoid the PICT format, which tends to print unreliably on high-resolution PostScript devices, and PCX files, which can't save CMYK information for color separations. Both TIFF and EPS file formats offer several variant options, which make each

File Format	File Extension	Recommended Output Media	Special Advantages	Potential Disadvantages
TIFF	.tif	Print	Efficient file size Can save alpha channels Can save color separations in a single file	Prints CMYK files more slowly than EPS format Can't save duotones
EPS	.eps, .epsf	Print	Can save duotone information Can save alpha channels Can save clipping paths Can save color separations in 1 or 5 files Can embed screening information and tone curves directly in the file	Preview cumbersome and adds to file size Five-file color separations hard to keep track of
Scitex CT	.ct	Print	For output by high-end Scitex color prepress systems	Can't save channels or paths
PICT	.pict, .pct	Multimedia, presentations, video	Compact file size Can include both raster and vector information	Unreliable for printing Not supported by some PC-compatible applications
BMP	.bmp	Multimedia, presentations, video	Compatible with most Windows applications	Not supported by many Macintosh applications
TARGA	.tga	Multimedia, presentations, video	Can save alpha channel information	Not supported by many Macintosh applications

Table 9–1

File Format Reference

format best suited for specific uses. We'll discuss these options in the sections that follow.

TIFF (.tif)

The TIFF (Tagged Image File Format) format was developed specifically for use in page layout applications. All major image-editing, painting, and page-composition packages support it, and it's readable on multiple platforms.

Several variants of TIFF exist, but most major software applications support the latest, version 6.0. You can save bitmap, grayscale, RGB color, CMYK color, and CIELAB color images (but not duotones) as TIFF files. The TIFF format offers several convenient advantages. You can

- Save alpha channel information in applications that support it.

- Compress a file using LZW (Lempel-Ziv-Welch) encoding, which is a *lossless* type of compression that doesn't destroy any data or degrade image quality. LZW compression compresses data by only a 2:1 factor.

- Save the file for use on a specific platform (PC and Macintosh variants of TIFF place data in a different order). Most major page layout applications can open TIFFs created for either platform; but when in doubt, save TIFFs for the platform on which the page layout software will be used.

Figure 9–1 shows TIFF save options in Adobe Photoshop.

When you save a CMYK image in TIFF format, it's considered *preseparated*. Most major page layout applications now support automatic color separation of imported CMYK TIFF images. Before converting an RGB TIFF image to CMYK mode, though, make sure you've set up

color separation information (UCR, GCR, and black generation) correctly for the press conditions of your job (you'll find more information about these in *Preparing Digital Images for Print*, the second book in this series). Otherwise, colors may not print as you expect.

Tip: *Many color houses and service bureaus prefer to receive preseparated CMYK files in the TIFF format because they are generally smaller and take less time to process through an imagesetter than an EPS file.*

EPS (.eps, .epsf)

The Encapsulated PostScript file format (abbreviated as .eps on the PC and as .epsf on the Macintosh) is another cross-platform standard. It was originally intended for saving vector drawings in a way that could be exported to other illustration applications or to a page layout, but the definition of the format has since widened to include raster images. Like TIFF, the EPS format is well suited to print output; but with its roots in PostScript, the EPS format can save additional types of information—making it preferable to TIFF in some situations (see Table 9–1). Save a file as EPS when you need to preserve the following kinds of information:

- Duotone, tritone, or quadtone curves
- Alpha channels (also possible with TIFF)
- Color separations (also possible with TIFF)
- Clipping paths
- Custom halftone screening and tonal curve information that apply only to a particular image, not to a printed document as a whole

Caution: *Unlike vector EPS images, raster EPS images can't be infinitely enlarged without the risk of degradation.*

Figure 9–2 shows the EPS format options available in Adobe Photoshop, which offers especially comprehensive support for controlling the way an EPS file prints. Let's take a brief look at some of these options and how they affect the information in an EPS file.

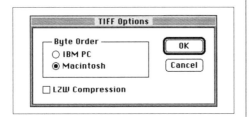

Figure 9–1

Options for saving a TIFF file in Adobe Photoshop

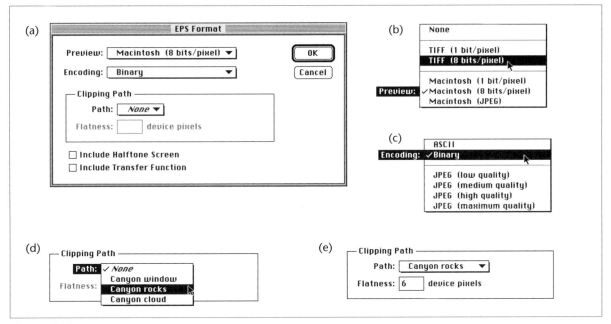

Figure 9–2
EPS file format options in Adobe Photoshop

Note: *EPS save options may vary from one application to another.*

Preview Options

EPS files consist of two parts—a PostScript-language description of the image, and a preview for placing the image correctly in another application. Previews (Figure 9–2b) can be black and white, 8-bit grayscale or color, or JPEG compressed color, but they're not entirely WYSIWYG. The type of preview you choose has a considerable effect on file size. Files with no preview are the smallest, but they're inconvenient to place, crop, or scale in another application because you have no visual reference. JPEG compressed previews (see the "Lossy Compression" section of this chapter) take up much less space than 8-bit previews, but not all applications support their use. EPS previews are in PICT format for Macintosh files and in TIFF format for PC-platform files.

DCS EPS Options

The DCS file options shown in Figure 9-3 apply only if you're saving a CMYK color file in the EPS format. Developed by Quark, Inc., the Desktop Color Separation (DCS) variant of the EPS file format allows you to embed color separation information within the file. The original version of DCS, version 1.0, creates five separate files—a color or grayscale preview (Figure 9–3) and four other files representing the data in each color plate (Figure 9–4). The more recent DCS version 2.0 saves all color separation information in a single file. Opinions vary about which type of DCS format to use. Some color houses, service bureaus, and production professionals still prefer the older, five-file type of DCS because the preview file is smaller and easier to manipulate in a layout. On the other hand, the single files created using DCS 2.0 are easier to keep track of, even if they consume more disk space and increase screen redraw time. Many prepress vendors claim that single-file DCS separations process through the image-setter more quickly than their five-file counterparts.

Encoding

This option (Figure 9–2c) affects the coding of the actual image data in the file. ASCII plain-text encoding creates the largest file but is compatible with all platforms and output devices. Binary is smaller and faster, but may be incompatible with some PC-based software applications. JPEG compressed encoding is supported only by PostScript Level 2 printers and imagesetters. If you're outputting to an older PostScript Level 1 imagesetter or printer, use binary or ASCII encoding instead.

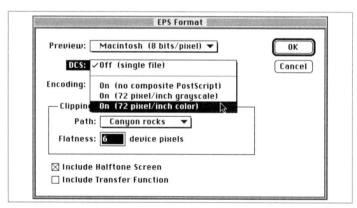

Figure 9–3

DCS Save options include a choice of single- or five-file format and the type of preview file that will be generated for five-file separations.

Clipping Path

By default, image files are always surrounded by a rectangular *bounding box*. If you want an irregular shape to print with a transparent background, you must use an image-editing package to create a *clipping path*—a mask around the irregular shape—and then export the image as an EPS file. When the EPS file is placed in a page layout or illustration, the background around the irregular shape drops out. Only the EPS file format supports the use of clipping paths (Figure 9–2d and e).

Some image-editing programs also let you define the *flatness* of the curves that make up the clipping path. This setting is for printing purposes. If the flatness setting is too low (say, 0 or 1), the clipping path curve is extremely smooth but might overload PostScript with too many control points and cause printing errors. If you set flatness too high, the curve will certainly print on any device, but its shape may look jagged. As a general rule of thumb, set flatness to 2 or 3 for low-resolution printers and to 6 or 8 for high-resolution imagesetters.

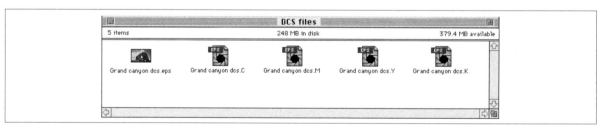

Figure 9–4

Saving an image in the DCS 1.0 EPS format generates five separate files—a preview file and one preseparated file for each color plate. The filenames for the separated colors include a one-letter suffix that indicates the color for that plate.

Halftone Screens and Transfer Functions

The EPS format also gives you the options of embedding halftone screening and transfer function settings in an image file (Figure 9–2a). A file saved with embedded halftone screen angle and frequency settings will output at those settings, regardless of how the operator of the page layout software or imagesetter tries to alter them. Embedding halftone screening in a file is useful when you want one image to print differently from other images in the document, or when you want to generate special patterning effects using low screen frequencies. *Transfer functions* have to do with custom gamma curves (see Chapter 7) that compensate for dot gain on an image-by-image basis. These expert settings are of greater interest to color prepress house staff and imagesetter operators than to designers.

Caution: *Embedding transfer functions in a file can override the calibration (or linearization) of an imagesetter's raster image processor (RIP) and is therefore not advisable unless the output device has not been calibrated.*

Scitex CT (.ct)

The Scitex Continuous Tone (CT) file format is proprietary to dedicated color prepress systems manufactured by Scitex. Save in this format only if you'll be transferring files to a Scitex system for layout and color separation. Scitex CT images can't retain any alpha channel or clipping path information.

Note: *Prepress industry consortiums are pushing for changes in major file formats that, if adopted, will make it possible to embed color management tag information in a file and transfer that information across platforms. See Chapter 5 for more about color management.*

File Formats for Multimedia, Presentations, Video, and Online Documents

The most popular file formats for images that will be output to media other than print are PICT on the Macintosh and BMP and TARGA on the IBM. If you'll be using a scanned image for both print and multimedia, be sure to save at least two versions of the file—one in TIFF or EPS for print output and another in the format best suited to the nonprint medium.

PICT (.pict, .pct)

The PICT file format, used primarily in Macintosh applications, is a standard in many multimedia authoring, presentation, and digital video-editing programs (including Adobe Persuasion, Adobe Premiere, Macromedia Director, and Microsoft PowerPoint). Save images in this format if you'll be exporting them to one of these programs or for output to a medium other than print.

PICT files can contain both vector and raster data. The format supports black and white, grayscale, and RGB color modes (but not CMYK color or duotones). JPEG compression for PICT files is an option in some applications—make sure the software to which you'll be exporting the image can open a compressed PICT.

BMP (.bmp)

The Windows Bitmap (BMP) file format was developed for compatibility with all Windows applications. OS/2 applications have their own version of BMP, and BMP files are accepted by many multimedia authoring, presentation, and digital video-editing programs on both the PC and Macintosh platforms. You can save black and white, grayscale, index color, and RGB color (but not duotones or CMYK color) images as BMP files.

TARGA (.tga)

TrueVision developed the TARGA file format for use in its high-end paint and video authoring applications, still in common use on the PC platform. The TARGA format can save grayscale and RGB color images at color depths of 16, 24, and 32 bits. A 32-bit TARGA file can contain alpha channel information.

Compression Dos and Don'ts

Color depth and scanning resolution both impact file size (see Chapters 5 and 7). Professionals who scan in color, or who scan critical technical and scientific documents in line art mode at high resolutions for archival purposes, are well aware of the drain on storage space that scanning causes. Increasingly, users of scanning products are turning to file or disk compression schemes as a solution for storing those ever-growing files.

File compression schemes fall into two general categories: *lossy* and *lossless*. Lossless compression schemes pack the data in a file without actually deleting information, so there's no loss to image detail, color, or output quality. Lossy compression solutions jettison data in user-definable amounts; the higher the compression ratio, the greater the potential for loss of image quality.

Lossless Compression Options

Commonly used nonlossy compression schemes include compression utilities and TIFF compression formats. Compression utilities compress all types of files without altering the original file format. TIFF compression options, on the other hand, are used exclusively with image files.

Compression Utilities

Disk and file compression utilities achieve smaller file sizes by making the best possible use of the hard drive or other physical storage medium. On the Macintosh, StuffIt and DiskDoubler are the standard file compression utilities, with DiskDoubler also offering compression for entire drives. On the PC, Stacker and Microsoft DoubleSpace offer disk compression, while PKZIP and LHARC are the most commonly used file compression utilities.

The degree of image file compression you can obtain through nonlossy utilities varies according to image color depth. Bitmap image files pack down more compactly than grayscales, and grayscales compress better than color files. Compression for color images rarely reaches a ratio greater than 2:1, with somewhat higher ratios possible for grayscale and line art files.

The greatest advantage to using general-purpose disk and file compression utilities is that they don't degrade image quality. On the downside, such utilities aren't compatible across platforms (limiting their practicality for file exchange); they offer limited savings in file size; and more time is required to open, save, and close the files they compress.

TIFF Compression Options

Some compression standards have been built into the various versions of the TIFF file format. The LZW (Lempel-Ziv-Welch) compression option described earlier in this chapter is supported by many major image-editing packages and achieves an average compression ratio of approximately 2:1. Many OCR and business communications packages feature TIFF PackBits, a compression option that applies to bitmap (black-and-white) TIFF files only.

Lossy Compression

If 2:1 compression ratios just aren't high enough, consider JPEG. JPEG stands for the Joint Photographic Experts Group, which developed this compression standard. JPEG compression ratios are user selectable in the host software and range from 2:1 (a true lossless type of compression) to about 40:1. In some software packages, such as Adobe Photoshop (Figure 9-2c), you can't choose a specific compression ratio but instead must pick a quality level. As the compression ratio increases (or the quality level decreases) and the resulting file becomes smaller, more data in the image is thrown away.

When you save an image using a JPEG algorithm, compression takes place within 8×8-pixel cells. The algorithm compares the similarity of color values within each cell and stores only those values that are relatively dissimilar. (The higher the level of compression you choose, the broader the range of color values that are considered similar, and the higher the number of color values that are thrown out.) When you reopen and decompress the file, the algorithm assigns a single color value to all the pixels in each cell that had similar color values before.

There's an ongoing debate about how much data loss is acceptable with JPEG compression. At what point does an image visibly degrade in quality? Although the results of high levels of compression are visible at very high magnifications, degradation is rarely obvious at actual size. Some industry professionals have suggested a compression ratio of 10:1 (roughly equal to a "Medium" Image Quality setting in Photoshop) as the threshold beyond which loss of quality becomes apparent. Images vary a great deal, so don't take anyone's word. Experiment with your own typical images before making a decision.

There are two factors—color content and original scanning resolution—that can help you predict how much JPEG compression a given image can stand. If the details of interest in an image are composed of blocks of solid color, then you can use a fairly high compression ratio and still not notice much change because color values in the image were similar to begin with. If an image is smoothly continuous in tone, on the other hand, a high compression ratio is likely to wipe out important gradations and result in jaggies or a visible loss of detail. By the same token, an image scanned at a high resolution can withstand a higher level of compression than one scanned at low resolution because it contains a broader range of color values per linear inch.

Tip: *It's okay to save JPEG-compressed images more than once, as long as you use the same compression ratio each time. Serious quality loss occurs only when you vary the compression ratio at each save, causing the algorithm to jettison more and more data and make mellow mincemeat out of what was once a coherent image.*

Appendix A: Vendors

Color Management/ Calibration Aids

ColorMatch, Colorimeter 24

DayStar Digital
5556 Atlanta Highway
Flowery Branch, GA 30542
Tel.: (800) 962-2077
Fax: (404) 967-3018

ColorMatch, Device Color Profile Starter Pack, Photoshop Acquire Module, Precision Input Color Characterization, Windows 95 Color Matching Module

Kodak Color Management Systems
343 State Street
Rochester, NY 14650
Tel.: (800) 75-COLOR, (716) 724-4000
Faxback options available

ColorSync 2.0

Apple Computer, Inc.
1 Infinite Loop
Cupertino, CA 95014
Tel.: (800) 767-2775
Fax: (800) 776-2333

ColorTron

Light Source Computer Images Inc.
17 East Sir Francis Drake Blvd., Suite 100
Larkspur, CA 94939
Tel.: (800) 994-COLOR
Fax: (415) 461-8090

EfiColor Works

Electronics for Imaging
2855 Campus Drive
San Mateo, CA 94403
Tel.: (415) 286-8617
Fax: (415) 358-9500

FotoTune

Agfa Division of Bayer Corporation
200 Ballardvale Street
Wilmington, MA 01887
Tel.: (617) 661-7900
Fax: (617) 661-0024

MonacoColor

Monaco Systems
100 Burtt Road, Suite 110
Andover, MA 01810
Tel.: (508) 749-9944
Fax: (508) 749-9977

Radius/SuperMatch Display Calibrator

Radius, Inc.
215 Moffett Park Drive
Sunnyvale, CA 94089
Tel.: (408) 541-6100
Fax: (408) 541-6150

Digital Cameras

Crosfield 130, Crosfield 160

DuPont Printing & Publishing
Barley Mill Plaza, Bldg. 15, Rm. 2113
Wilmington, DE 19898-0015
Tel.: (302) 992-5326
Fax: (302) 892-8335

DCS 460

Eastman Kodak
343 State Street
Rochester, NY 14650-0405
Tel., faxback: (800) CD-KODAK, (716) 724-4000

Dicomed Digital Camera

Dicomed
12270 Nicollett Avenue
Burnsville, MN 55337
Tel.: (612) 895-3000
Fax: (612) 895-3258

E2 and E2s series cameras

Nikon Electronic Imaging
1300 Walt Whitman Road
Melville, NY 11747
Tel.: (516) 547-4355
Fax: (516) 547-0305

QuickTake 150

Apple Computer, Inc.
1 Infinite Loop
Cupertino, CA 95014
Tel.: (800) 767-2775
Fax: (800) 776-2333

Image-Editing and Post-Processing Software

Adobe Photoshop

Adobe Systems, Inc.
1585 Charleston Road, P.O. Box 7900
Mountain View, CA 94039-7900
Tel.: (415) 961-4400
Fax: (415) 961-3769

Collage

Specular International
479 West Street
Amherst, MA 01002
Tel.: (800) 433-7732
Fax: (413) 253-0540

Convolver, Live Picture, Kai's Power Tools

HSC Software
6303 Carpinteria Avenue
Carpinteria, CA 93013
Tel.: (805) 566-6200
Fax: (805) 566-6385

Fractal Design Painter

Fractal Design Corporation
335 Spreckels Drive
Aptos, CA 95003
Tel.: (408) 688-8800
Fax: (408) 688-8836

Intellihance Pro RGB/CMYK

DPA Software
913 Baxter Drive
Plano, TX 75025
Tel.: (214) 517-6876
Fax: (214) 517-2354

Picture Publisher

Micrografx Corporation
1303 Arapaho
Richardson, TX 75081
Tel.: (800) 272-3729
Fax: (214) 234-2410

ScanPrepPro

ImageXpress, Inc.
1121 Casa Nova Ct.
Lawrenceville, GA 30244
Tel.: (404)564-9924
Fax: (404) 564-1632

Image Management

Fetch

Adobe Systems, Inc.
1585 Charleston Road, P.O. Box 7900
Mountain View, CA 94039-7900
Tel.: (415) 961-4400
Fax: (415) 961-3769

Kudo Image Browser

Imspace Systems Corp.
4747 Morena Blvd., Suite 360
San Diego, CA 92117
Tel.: (800) 949-4555
Fax: (619) 272-4292

Shoebox

Eastman Kodak
343 State Street
Rochester, NY 14650-0405
Tel., faxback: (800) CD-KODAK, (716) 724-4000

Image Storage

RCD-1000 Rewritable CD 650MB

Pinnacle Micro
19 Technology Drive
Irvine, CA 92718
Tel.: (800) 553-7070
Fax: (714) 789-9155

SB-TMO-1300 1.3MB MO drive

Micronet Technology
80 Technology Drive
Irvine, CA 92718
Tel.: (714) 453-6000
Fax: (714) 453-6001

SledgeHammer array drives

FWB Systems, Inc.
1555 Adams Drive
Menlo Park, CA 94025
Tel.: (415) 833-4604
Fax: (415) 833-4657

SyQuest 270MB removable drive system

SyQuest Technologies
47071 Bayside Parkway
Fremont, CA 94538
Tel.: (800) 245-2278
Fax: (510) 226-4102

Photo CD

Master Photo CD, Pro Photo CD, Print Photo CD, Portfolio Photo CD, Catalog Photo CD

Eastman Kodak
343 State Street
Rochester, NY 14650
Tel., faxback: (800) CD-KODAK, (716) 724-4000

Scanners, Drum

Chromagraph 3900

Linotype-Hell
425 Oser Avenue
Hauppauge, NY 11788
Tel.: (800) 842-9721
Fax: (516) 434-2706

ColorGetter III series scanners

Optronics
7 Stuart Rd.
Chelmsford, MA 01824
Tel.: (800) 331-7568
Fax: (508) 256-1872

Crosfield C6200

DuPont Printing & Publishing
Barley Mill Plaza, Bldg. 15, Rm. 2113
Wilmington, DE 19898-0015
Tel.: (302) 992-5326
Fax: (302) 892-8335

DT-1045AI, DT-1015AI

Screen USA
5110 Tollview Drive
Rolling Meadows, IL 60008
Tel.: (708) 870-7400
Fax: (708) 870-0149

ICG 350i series

ICG North America
113 Main Street
Hackettstown, NJ 07840
Tel.: (908) 813-1838
Fax: (908) 813-1676

PowerScan 4000

Birmy Graphics Corporation
250 East Drive, Suite H
Melbourne, FL 32904
Tel.: (407) 768-6766
Fax: (407) 768-9669

ScanMaster 4500

Howtek, Inc.
21 Park Avenue
Hudson, NH 03051
Tel.: (800) 444-6983
Fax: (603) 880-3843

Scanners, Film/Transparency

Crosfield C360

DuPont Printing & Publishing
Barley Mill Plaza, Bldg. 15, Rm. 2113
Wilmington, DE 19898-0015
Tel.: (302) 992-5326
Fax: (302) 892-8335

Leafscan 45

Scitex
8 Oak Park Drive
Bedford, MA 01730
Tel.: (617) 275-5150
Fax: (617) 275-3430

ScanMaker 45T

Microtek Lab
3715 Doolittle Drive
Redondo Beach, CA 90278
Tel.: (310) 297-5000
Fax: (310) 297-5050

SprintScan 35

Polaroid Imaging Peripheral Systems
565 Technology Square, Suite 3C
Cambridge, MA 02174
Tel.: (800) 432-5335
Fax: (617) 386-3584

SuperCoolscan

Nikon Electronic Imaging
1300 Walt Whitman Road
Melville, NY 11747
Tel.: (516) 547-4355
Fax: (516) 547-0305

Vision 35

Agfa Division of Bayer Corporation
200 Ballardvale Street
Wilmington, MA 01887
Tel.: (617) 661-7900
Fax: (617) 661-0024

Scanners, Flatbed/Sheetfed

Horizon Plus, SelectScan

Agfa Division of Bayer Corporation
200 Ballardvale Street
Wilmington, MA 01887
Tel.: (617) 661-7900
Fax: (617) 661-0024

ProImager 8000

Pixelcraft, Inc.
130 Doolittle Drive, Suite 19
San Leandro, CA 94577
Tel.: (800) 933-0330
Fax: (510) 562-6451

Smart 730

Scitex
8 Oak Park Drive
Bedford, MA 01730
Tel.: (617) 275-5150
Fax: (617) 275-3430

Topaz

Linotype-Hell
425 Oser Avenue
Hauppauge, NY 11788
Tel.: (800) 842-9721
Fax: (516) 434-2706

UMAX PowerLook, PageOffice

UMAX
3353 Gateway Blvd.
Fremont, CA 94538
Tel.: (800) 562-0311
Fax: (510) 651-8834

ScanMaster 2500

Howtek, Inc.
21 Park Avenue
Hudson, NH 03051
Tel.: (800) 444-6983
Fax: (603) 880-3843

ScanMaker III

Microtek Lab
3715 Doolittle Drive
Redondo Beach, CA 90278
Tel.: (310) 297-5000
Fax: (310) 297-5050

Index

Draw on Our Expertise

Announcing the first book published on CorelDRAW!™ 6 under the new *CorelPRESS* imprint

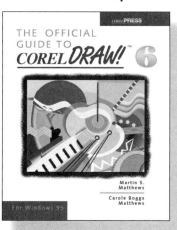

The Official Guide to CorelDRAW!™6 for Windows 95
by Martin S. Matthews and
Carole Boggs Matthews
$34.95, U.S.A., ISBN: 0-07-882168-1
Available October, 1995

It's here...the only OFFICIAL book on CorelDRAW!™6 for Windows 95! Featuring full-color illustrations, it's packed with step-by-step instructions for creating award-winning artwork, as well as insider tips and techniques from the staff at Corel. In addition, answers to all of the most frequently asked tech support questions are here — no phone call needed. It's all here in *The Official Guide to CorelDRAW!™6 for Windows 95.*

ORDER TODAY!

Oracle Power Objects Handbook
by Bruce Kolste and
David Petersen
$29.95, U.S.A.
ISBN: 0-07-882089-8
Available August, 1995

Digital Images: A Practical Guide
by Adele Droblas Greenberg and Seth Greenberg
$24.95, U.S.A.
ISBN: 0-07-882113-4
Available September, 1995

LAN Times Guide to Multimedia Networking
by Nancy Cox,
Charles T. Manley, Jr.,
and Francis E. Chea
$29.95, U.S.A.
ISBN: 0-07-882114-2
Available August, 1995

Peachtree Accounting for Windows Made Easy: The Basics & Beyond!
by John Hedtke
$29.95, U.S.A.
ISBN: 0-07-882127-4
Available Now

OSBORNE

BC640SL

ORDER BOOKS DIRECTLY FROM OSBORNE/McGRAW-HILL

For a complete catalog of Osborne's books, call 510-549-6600 or write to us at 2600 Tenth Street, Berkeley, CA 94710

☎ **Call Toll-Free:** *1-800-822-8158*
24 hours a day, 7 days a week in U.S. and Canada

✉ **Mail this order form to:**
McGraw-Hill, Inc.
Customer Service Dept.
P.O. Box 547
Blacklick, OH 43004

📠 **Fax this order form to:**
1-614-759-3644

💻 **EMAIL**
7007.1531@COMPUSERVE.COM
COMPUSERVE GO MH

Ship to:

Name _____

Company _____

Address _____

City / State / Zip _____

Daytime Telephone: _____
(We'll contact you if there's a question about your order.)

ISBN #	BOOK TITLE	Quantity	Price	Total
0-07-88				
0-07-88				
0-07-88				
0-07-88				
0-07-88				
0-07088				
0-07-88				
0-07-88				
0-07-88				
0-07-88				
0-07-88				
0-07-88				
0-07-88				

Shipping & Handling Charge from Chart Below	
Subtotal	
Please Add Applicable State & Local Sales Tax	
TOTAL	

Shipping & Handling Charges

Order Amount	U.S.	Outside U.S.
Less than $15	$3.50	$5.50
$15.00 - $24.99	$4.00	$6.00
$25.00 - $49.99	$5.00	$7.00
$50.00 - $74.99	$6.00	$8.00
$75.00 - and up	$7.00	$9.00

Occasionally we allow other selected companies to use our mailing list. If you would prefer that we not include you in these extra mailings, please check here: ☐

METHOD OF PAYMENT

☐ Check or money order enclosed (payable to Osborne/McGraw-Hill)

☐ AMERICAN EXPRESS   ☐ DISCOVER   ☐ MasterCard   ☐ VISA

Account No. ☐☐☐☐☐☐☐☐☐☐☐☐☐☐☐☐

Expiration Date _____

Signature _____

In a hurry? Call 1-800-822-8158 anytime, day or night, or visit your local bookstore.

Thank you for your order

Code BC640SL